The People's Culture

Published by Mazda Motor Corporation
Hiroshima, Japan

The People's Culture
from Kyoto to Edo

Edited by Yoshida Mitsukuni, Tanaka Ikko and Sesoko Tsune

Covers:
A bridge taken from a section of an eight-panel screen of Edo in the early 17th century. At this time, Edo was already a burgeoning city following its establishment in 1600 as the administrative capital of Japan under the Shogun Tokugawa Ieyasu. This bridge is one that connects the main city with reclaimed land that was designated as an entertainment district including theaters, amusement quarters and bathhouses. In the Edo period, the city abounded with rivers and canals that were crossed by more than 270 bridges. The bridges were designed with accented curves to allow the flow of boats that were the principal means of transport for both people and commerce. Bridges also served a security function, separating Edo's many semi-autonomous administrative sections.

Inside Covers:
Scenes from the same screen from which the bridge on the cover was taken.
The inside front cover shows samurai, merchants and priests (center) enjoying an puppet show to the accompaniment of music. In the center foreground are rooms that serve as teahouses, a standard appurtenance to theaters of the time. Behind the audience in the center are the balcony seats.
The inside back cover also shows a theatrical performance, this one a Noh play dedicated to the spirits. The stage is at right center, with the walkway leading to the stage in the foreground. The theater itself is located outside the Kanda Myōjin Shrine whose entrance gate (center) and *torii* (upper left) can be seen. In the center foreground is a three-tiered pagoda.

The Japanese names in this book are given last name first in the customary Japanese order.

Contents

Text by Yoshida Mitsukuni

The Wellsprings of Japanese Culture——Yoshida Mitsukuni

The world as Japanese saw it in early times was first depicted in map form in the beginning of the eighth century. It was a finite world consisting only of the main island stretching from east to west and a few smaller islands in the periphery, all surrounded by a vast ocean. This conception is believed to be the work of a Buddhist monk named Gyōki (668-749).

It is not particularly unusual that Gyōki was also a cartographer, for the Buddhist orders were the best-educated members of society at the time, and, in addition to propagating their religion they took a leading role in educating the people throughout Japan. They had wide engineering and architectural know-how, and built irrigation reservoirs and canals all over the country, constructed roads, and built bridges. Even today there are bridges preserved that legend holds were originally built by the priest Gyōki. The Buddhist clergy of Japan played a role comparable to that of the Frères Pontifes of thirteenth-century Europe, the Christian brotherhood that was responsible for the building of many famous bridges, including the Pont Saint Ésprit over the Rhone river and the Pont Saint Bénézet over the Avignon.

There is little documentary evidence of the activities of Gyōki, but a copy of his map, which was made in 1305, has been preserved, and this is the oldest known example of the so-called Gyōki-type map of Japan as a whole. This depiction was the accepted form of the Japanese archipelago until as late as the seventeenth century. At its center is a province called Yamashiro no kuni, where Kyoto, then the capital of the country, was located.

Later versions of the Gyōki map have the names Daitoku, Rasetsu-koku, and Gando added around the periphery of Japan. Daitoku meant China, a name that reflected its status as the august, advanced nation of the time. But the other names—Rasetsu-koku and Gando—suggest realms inhabited by demons and curious creatures. For the ancient Japanese, everything outside the world with which they had concrete contact was the abode only of monstrous and inhuman creatures.

The same was true, however, of the Europeans' image of the world from around the sixth century to medieval times. In Europe of the Greek and Roman eras, there was already a fairly high level of scientific knowledge of geography. Herodotus (5th century B.C.) had recorded the world according to his own experience in his great *History,* and Erathosthenes (B.C. 276-196) and Ptolemy had extremely broad knowledge of the world. Ptolemy's world map centered on the Mediterranean Sea; like Gyōki, he put the familiar realm at the center, and called the unknown realms at either end Terra Incognita and Fortunatae Insulae.

In the medieval age, the center of the European world became the sacred land Jerusalem. Surrounding the flat continent was a vast ocean, Oceanus. Paradise lay at the eastern edge of the world and from that direction flowed four rivers, the Nile, the Indus, the Tigris, and the Euphrates. The world was divided into three: Asia, Africa, and Europe. In addition to Jerusalem, the cities of

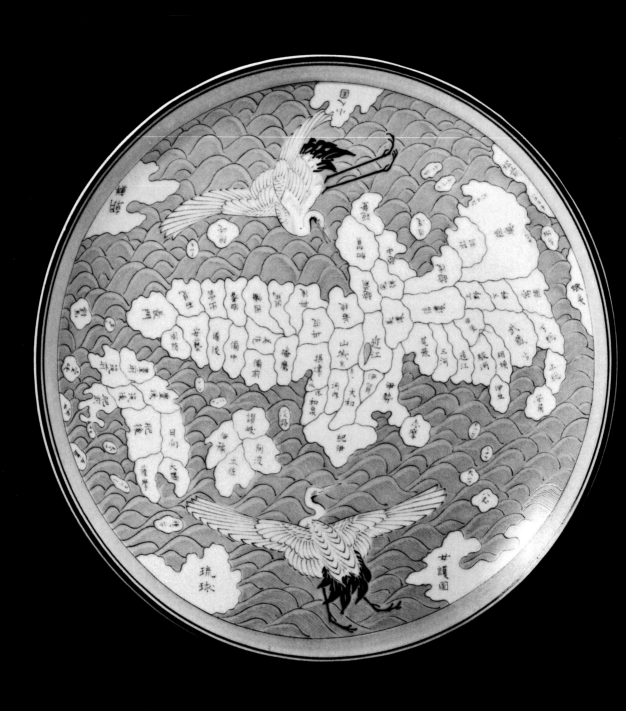

The Buddhist monk Gyōki who drew this map placed Yamashiro (Kyoto) at the center of Japan.

Rome, Bethlehem, Alexandria, and Carthage were marked, as were the Pyrenees and Alps mountain ranges, the Danube, Rhine, and other rivers. However, everything beyond this world was believed to be the abode of monstrous, alien life, the habitation of headless or one-eyed men, long-legged giants, men with dog's heads and so on—the world of Gog and Magog as described in the Book of Revelations. All these creatures, along with Satan himself, were the terrifying beings that could bring the world to an end.

The ancient Chinese, too, had a clearly defined world. In a geography believed to have been compiled around the 3rd century B.C. entitled the *Shan-hai-ching*, the western edge of the world was bounded by high mountains that were shown as the abode of two supreme deities named Hsi Wang Mu and Tung Wang Fu. The mountain where Hsi Wang Mu resided was a beautiful, Eden-like paradise where the peaches of eternal youth and immortality and the elixir of life were to be found. But the realm beyond China itself was believed to be populated by weird and monstrous creatures. Just as the ancient Europeans imagined them, they included one-eyed men, headless creatures with eyes and mouths in their torsos, men with knees that bent forward, men with deeply set eyes, huge ears, enlarged feet or heels, and giants. In addition there were myriad deities of fantastic visage; the nine-tailed god with a human head and the body of a tiger, a winged creature with a human head and a horse's body, and a monster with a snake's body and nine human heads. There were human figures spouting fire, with oddly-protruding chests, with wings, with cavities in their chests, with three heads on one body and with forked tongues and all manner of other hideous and frightening forms.

The world of human beings was thought by the Chinese to be confined to the domain over which the emperor, who had received the mandate of heaven to rule on earth, reigned. It extended, therefore, only from the Yellow River on the north to the banks of the Yangtze in the central part of the continent, and the center of this world was the emperor. This concept of the world became established quite early in history, and maps for practical use existed in China from some time around the beginning of the Christian era. The concepts of scale, direction, and distance were well known by the third century, and in 801 a map of the Chinese world was compiled after gathering together all information on geography available at the time. The scale of this map is about 1/1,500,000 and it includes lines of latitude and longitude.

The peoples of ancient times all over the globe created images of the world they knew and in which they lived out of empirical experience and perceptions. Whatever lay outside of their experience was a purely conceptual world. The image of that world, in the case of Europe as well as Japan and China, was conceived and nurtured in a closed and self-contained system. Any world beyond immediate experience was necessarily seen as inhuman and fantastic.

Just as the center of Gyōki's map of Japan was the capital city of Kyoto, the centers of the

This map published in the 12th century places Jerusalem at the center of a world then still believed to be flat.

Western worlds surrounded by Oceanus were the ancient cities of Jerusalem and Carthage or the medieval metropolises of Rome and Paris. One might say that the abstract world as it was conceived by man, which was independent and culturally homogenous, was made into concrete and empirical experience through the reality of the cities. People from all parts of Japan came to the city of Kyoto, and it became the wellspring and source of all news and information. In the same way, it was said that "all roads lead to Rome," and Rome became the great pivot of culture in the European world. In Japan, a journey to the capital of Kyoto, then called Heiankyō, was the opportunity to experience a city conceived of as Utopia. For the European, a pilgrimage to Rome was the realization of the people's yearning to touch the fountainhead of culture.

Kyoto, built in the late eighth century, was modeled after the ancient Chinese capitals of Loyang and Chang-an, and is famous for its Chinese-style principles of city planning. The city is roughly square in plan with a wide boulevard 85 meters wide and 1,280 meters long running down its north-south axis. All the other large and small streets are either parallel or perpendicular to this axis. The large main boulevard is used for city festivals, parades and other such purposes. The ideal image of the city as well as its geometrical symmetry had begun to erode by around the twelfth century, but the grid of large and small streets remains the basic framework of the city, with the imperial palace as its focal point even to this day.

It was here in the city of Kyoto that the aristocratic culture centered around the emperor grew and flourished. In the early Heian period, Japan took the advanced and sophisticated China as its model not only in city planning, but in many other aspects of culture. The emperor, the bureaucracy, as well as the nobility, many of whom were also government officials, enjoyed a gracious style of living copied after that of the Chinese aristocracy. The trappings of their elegant lifestyle were created and furnished by officially-run workshops. The nobles and high-ranking officials who used the products of these workshops, moreover, expected highly refined techniques and designs that reflected the seasonal changes of the Japanese landscape.

In a papermaking shop in the Heian period, there might be four artisans involved in production. During the longest days of the year between April and July, they would make an average of 196 sheets per worker per day. During the shortest days from October to January, the daily average was about 125 per person. The annual average was roughly 168 sheets a day, quite a modest, certainly not excessive, output. In a silversmith's workshop, the work was subdivided among specialists in casting, polishing, rim-making and so on. Workers were paid in kind in the form of rice and salt. Indeed, records tell us, an urban production system, with specialization among professional artisans, prescribed production outputs, and the practice of pay in accordance with work was relatively well established by the ninth or tenth centuries.

Efficiently served by this system of production, the nobility of ancient Japan ordered articles to suit their specific needs and tastes. In the course of learning how to fulfill the demands of their discriminating clients, the artisans began to make articles that were deemed even better than the artifacts imported from China after which they were modeled. The Japanese nobility treasured and appreciated fine works of art and used them to increase even more the beauty of their surroundings. During this period, the court nobility played the role of art director, so to speak, while the artisans—the ordinary people—strove to respond to their demands. *The Tale of Genji*, the great work of fiction depicting the life and psychology of the court nobility written in the tenth century, contains many passages describing daily life at the court and the articles they used, made to order to suit their idiosyncratic tastes. The court nobility lived out their entire lives within the city of Kyoto, and Kyoto alone was the real world for them. Everything—their religion and literature, their diversions and paintings—all were created out of the landscape and by the people of that city.

At the end of the twelfth century, Kyoto ceased to be the center of political authority. Power passed from the hands of the nobility and the bureaucracy to the rising warrior class, and the headquarters of government was moved to Kamakura, a town south of present-day Tokyo. But Kyoto, with the imperial palace at its heart, continued to be the pivot of culture. The nobility retained leadership in the cultural realm, and even the new military leaders of the country took aristocratic standards as their guide in establishing their own culture. The warriors wore leather armor laced with variegated colors of thread, and the color combinations they used faithfully followed the rules of color combination fashionable in the kimonos of the court ladies. The decorative ornaments attached to their armor, moreover, were much like the fittings found on furnishings in the homes of the nobility. Warrior etiquette was also set in imitation of the manners of the courtier class.

The emergence of new political leaders in eastern Japan whose lifestyle, in contrast to that of the nobility, was based on the realistic struggle for survival through military prowess, proved a powerful force of change. Gyōki's map had made Kyoto the hub of Japan's world, but from the end of the twelfth century, that world became polarized between the old capital of Kyoto in the west, led by the emperor and the nobility, and Kamakura in the east, under the new warrior elite. The character of these two centers of culture, moreover, was quite different. The former sought to create an ideal world. The clearest example of this was their favorite pastime, the writing of short poems. Every aspect of culture or sentiment was expressed in poetic form, and that the poems were not only extremely abstract and symbolic but compacted into verses composed of five lines and thirty-one characters. By contrast, the way of life of the warrior was typified by action and realism, and he placed the concrete, the functional, and the practical above all else. Warrior-class culture was a response to those values, but in the end it was forced to turn to the conventions of the nobility for models as it underwent the process of systematization and stylization.

Meanwhile, the culture of Kyoto in the age after the city ceased to be the political center grew gradually more dense, condensed, and introspective. This tendency was strengthened by the popularity of the philosophy of the Chinese sage Chu Hsi and then again under the influence of Zen Buddhism. Chu Hsi's Confucianism stressed the importance of the individual and his internalized ethic and moral rectitude. In contrast to Confucianism as it had been previously taught, primarily as a political philosophy of the state, this school of thought treated the problems of the individual. The focus of Zen Buddhism was much the same. Buddhism as it had been first introduced to Japan was a religion intended for protection of the state, and the statue of the Great Buddha built at Nara, when it was the capital and the center of the country (710-94), was erected for that purpose. In the Heian period, the court nobility of Kyoto, led by the powerful Fujiwara clan, made Buddhism a private religion, centering on the institutions of the clan. Shut up in a confined and exclusive world, they built small shrines within their homes for Buddhist images to guard the fortunes of their own families or constructed temples to pray for the prosperity of the clan. Zen took Buddhism yet another step by demanding that the individual resolve all his questions throuth solitary meditation. This required concentrated thought. In time confirmation of the strength of the individual and his world became the primary goals of the culture of Kyoto.

Then, in the fourteenth century, the polarized culture of Japan was once again unified and its center returned to Kyoto. The political forces that had become established in eastern Japan did not wane, however, but continued to form a strong nucleus of power existing side-by-side with the Ashikaga shogun in Kyoto.

The warrior leaders who moved to Kyoto became the successors to the culture of the nobility, but unlike the nobility, they were not carried away by conceptual, ephemeral beauty. Through meditation, they searched for the transcendental existence of the Buddha within themselves and tried to live according to the rules and principles of action as taught by Zen. The warrior elite, moreover, rediscovered nature as the world of the Buddha. The beauty they learned to appreciate was different from the natural, seasonal beauties of the Kyoto landscape that so delighted the nobility. It was a beauty of the essence of nature.

When surrounded by the unchanging, eternal beauty of nature, human life is but a dream, an illusion. The Zen priests of the medieval period believed that reality was all illusion and fantasy, and many of their names included the character *mu* (dream) or *gen* (illusion). The titles of their writings, too, often include these words. They also sought to portray the ideas of Zen using the monochrome form of landscape painting (*suiboku-ga*) developed in Sung and Yüan China. This style of painting was not realistic, but inspired by the images of landscapes that emerged in the mind of painter—such works were reflections of the mental images that lay between reality and

Part of the Jurakudai Palace in Kyoto that Hideyoshi ordered his vassals to build. It was completed in 1586.

unreality. Devotees of Zen sought environments to surround themselves with that were not real, natural landscapes, but landscapes as seen in the mind's eye. They abstracted nature and created gardens that were symbolic of it. And in these abstractions they employed both the traditional love of nature and respect for stone that goes back to ancient times and the utopian thought of China with its belief in immortal beings who reside in high mountains.

These gardens could be enjoyed from inside or from the verandas of adjacent buildings, with their changes from season to season an eternal source of inspiration. The implication of such garden designs was freedom of perspective: every individual is free to see things his own way. The freedom to determine one's own standpoint, moreover, allowed a person to indulge in the pleasures of the world of illusion, and even to become completely intoxicated by it. The eccentrics who lost themselves among beautiful flowers and ideal landscapes until the human spirit was borne away, as it were, into an existence sustained only by dream and illusion were sometimes described as "mad," a state of spiritual rapture that was called *kyō*. Where man once achieved a trance-like state through the transcendental power of the gods or the Supreme, now he could gain it through beauty. In time, the dances and music once performed only before the transcendental being began to be performed before other human beings. The Noh drama developed. And the main characters in the Noh plays were beings who moved constantly back and forth between the real world and the world of illusion.

While Kyoto was enveloped in this world of dream and illusion, new forces of military power were rising up around the countryside. They were led by the sons of farmers who possessed a simple, rude, and very real armed strength. They sought real, not nominal, power over the country. And so from about the middle of the fifteenth century for about one-hundred years—the century known as the Sengoku or "the country at war" period, the struggle for supremacy among the many rival clans raged throughout the country.

Eventually, new leaders emerged. These men made skillful use of the arquebus, brought by the Portuguese to Japan in 1543 and quickly mass-produced locally, to equip their soldiers. With these invincible forces, they defeated the armies of rival chieftains armed only with antiquated spears and swords, finally attaining ultimate supremacy over the country. The new heroes of battle were the products of the countryside; they had no connection with the old aristocracy. But they went to Kyoto, which had retained the status of capital city of Japan, and secured legitimacy for their position as the new rulers of the country under the aegis of the emperor.

These new rulers, Oda Nobunaga (1534-82) and his successor Toyotomi Hideyoshi (1536-98) were firm realists, uncultivated and ruthless by nature. They rose to power through realistic means: vast armies and control of economic resources. And all of them built enormous castles. The Azuchi Castle built by Nobunaga was seven floors high and Hideyoshi's Osaka Castle had

This 17th century painting of Kyoto shows the affluence that merchants had attained by that time.

eight stories. Their interiors, moreover, were lavishly decorated with gilt and gorgeously colored paintings executed by the finest artists of the day. The style of the castles preserved today was basically established at this time.

In order to augment their economic resources, these sixteenth century leaders allowed the free market to flourish and encouraged merchants. As a result, cities rapidly grew up in those parts of the country where transportation and distribution routes converged. Gold and silver mines were developed and, as casting of coins became widespread, the currency economy gradually took root.

The capital of Kyoto, meanwhile, had been transformed. Beginning in 1549, Hideyoshi had permitted the Jesuits to propagate the Catholic faith and had allowed a church to be built in Kyoto. As a result, Japanese culture, which had developed over the centuries largely in isolation from the world, began to absorb influences from Western culture. Hideyoshi also built many new streets in the city of Kyoto and surrounded the whole with embankments in order to better fortify it, although these works were not particularly effective for defense. The construction of the grandiose Nijō castle and Jurakudai palace, both of which combined fortress and residence into one immense structure, also drastically changed the face of the city. The latter, in particular, was ostentatious to the extreme, even its roof tiles covered with gilt. The culture that had idealized dream and illusion turned about face; it was gripped by a passionate realism, and these values gradually began to permeate the urban populace. A kind of hero worship spread throughout the culture.

A tremendous change took place in the value systems of the city. In former times, the social class that was politically supreme had determined the value system of the culture of the city, and the townspeople had found their proper place in that system. This was the pattern that had governed the culture of Kyoto since the eighth century. However, with the advent of the era of heroism, the people had to construct their own value systems. The new rulers went about building a new cultural order based on a simple realism in their own rustic, direct fashion. Their sense of power radiated in all directions; their very dazzle and audacity fascinated people. As time went on, cultural spheres oriented to different sets of coordinates began to come into being. Cultural heroes in all walks of life created their own spheres of influence and established themselves upon a system of coordinates distinct from those of the rulers. In the sixteenth century, however, their spheres frequently overlapped with those of the persons in power. One example is Sen no Rikyū (1522-91), founder of one of the most influential schools of the tea ceremony, and his patron, Toyotomi Hideyoshi, who then held supreme power in Japan. Another is Hon'ami Kōetsu (1558-1637), artist, and calligrapher who was closely associated with Tokugawa Ieyasu (1542-1616), founder of the Tokugawa shogunate.

This woodblock print of warehouses and ships well describes the bustle of Osaka as a center of commerce and distribution.

The glory of each hero, however, was short-lived. No sooner did one pass from this world when a new hero would arise to take his place. Their coming and passing was a poignant reminder of the brevity of human life. Under such realistic leaders, the religious myth of eternity was cast aside. The "eternal truth" as taught by Zen was forgotten and lost. In its place, man affirmed the brevity of life and sought to live to the utmost in the brilliant reality of urban life. As one wealthy merchant said, there is no need to think about life after death until the age of fifty; and after all, life in the next world is unknowable to man. Nobunaga declared outright that another world simply did not exist and that there was no existence beyond what man could see with his own eyes. It was a time of affirmation of reality and of readiness to confirm human life by enjoying the reality of the secular world.

Then in the year 1600, Hideyoshi died and Tokugawa Ieyasu, who had solidified his position as successor to power, set up his headquarters in the city of Edo, present-day Tokyo. Once again, Japan became a world polarized between two major cities. Kyoto remained the seat of spiritual authority symbolized by the figure of the emperor. Edo became the headquarters of the shogun, the actual holder of political power and military hegemony. This dual structure of authority profoundly puzzled early foreign visitors to Japan. The way they finally explained it was that Edo was the seat of the secular ruler, while the emperor in Kyoto represented a spiritual sovereign like the Pope of Rome. Nevertheless Japan had not essentially changed; it was still the isolated world surrounded by ocean as Gyōki had depicted it. The same was still true then of Europe, too, where a great debate was raging as to whether the inhabitants of the New World whom Christopher Columbus had encountered were indeed human beings or not.

As the new political, economic, and military center, construction of the city of Edo progressed rapidly. It grew up around Edo castle, which was built where the Imperial Palace stands today. City planning followed a scheme dictated by military priorities. The residence of the shogun and the headquarters of the government were located in Edo castle. Land was set aside around it for the residences of the feudal lords, and housing areas for samurai families, merchants, and artisans lay in a yet wider circle. There was a tremendous ferment of building and internal movement in the city that went on for more than forty years.

In the meantime, the shogunate hastened to establish a stable system of feudal control over the country. The philosophy of Chu Hsi became the new political ideology. A clearly defined social system dividing the populace into four classes—samurai, peasant, artisan or merchant— was established. Kyoto became an economic center based on traditional handicraft industries and a center of high-brow culture pivoting on the nobility, the new leisure class now far removed from political power, and the low-brow or popular culture that had begun to flower in the medieval age. At least superficially, feudal society appeared stable. As the social system solidified, with the rulers, the samurai, on the one hand and the ruled, the townspeople and farmers, on the other, subcultures began to emerge and flourish within each stratum. The world of popular culture naturally expanded, for the population of peasants and townspeople was far greater than that of samurai.

In Kyoto, and Osaka—which was fast becoming a center of commerce along with Kyoto—numerous genre of traditional culture spread among the common people and in the process were further refined and diversified. The painters who followed the traditional school of painting in the Chinese-style catered to the tastes of the samurai class. And from among the townspeople, responding to the tastes of the urban population, emerged the *ukiyoe*. These woodblock prints were extremely popular among the townspeople both as a means of duplicating and distributing news and information, such as about plays being performed or fashions in vogue, and as a form of art. The same branching of culture occurred in other fields. Tanka poetry remained the favorite literary form of the court nobility, but it was little more than the pastime of the leisure class. The lead in the world of poetry was taken over by the realistic and witty *haikai*. These terse verses offered a ready form to enjoy parody and to find humor in the realities of human life. It was the great poet Matsuo Bashō (1644-94) who turned poetry toward the appreciation of nature and away from the doctrine of dream and illusion. The stratification of aesthetic values spread through every realm of culture and was sustained and nurtured by the new urban bourgeoisie.

In 1657 a great fire broke out in Edo, burning 60 percent of the city to ashes. Rebuilding began immediately, this time in accordance with a new plan for the city. Surrounding areas were simultaneously incorporated, in all totalling 933 districts or *chō*, which was three times as many as there had been in the early seventeenth century. In addition, the estates of the *daimyō* as well as many temples and shrines were distributed in various parts of the city and these became the nuclei of new development. Vacant areas were also set aside to serve as a fire-breaks.

In this way Edo became a vast metropolis with a population in the 1700s of about 1,200,000. In contemporary Europe, the largest city was London, with a population of 800,000, and the second largest Paris, with 500,000 people. Most of the Edo population was concentrated in the area set aside for the *chōnin*—the ordinary townspeople. It is estimated that there were 67,000 people per square kilometer, far more than the average population density of Tokyo today, so that Edo was filled with dense, slum-like areas surrounded by endless urban sprawl. By comparison, the population of Kyoto at this time was 250,000 and that of Osaka, 400,000.

In addition to these three great cities were smaller local cities pivoting on the castles built by each feudal lord. Most of the provincial cities of today trace their beginnings to these castle towns. Most of the castle towns were roughly similar to Edo in plan: the castle at its center, ringed with samurai residences, and surrounded by the homes of tradesmen and artisans. Farm villages clustered around the castle towns, but there was no wall between the rural countryside and the town itself. This is one important characteristic of Japanese cities. Castle walls in European cities were a culture's first line of defense. A castle wall generally meant that a homogeneous, closed-off cultural system was created within, while the world outside possessed its own, quite distinct culture. But in the case of Japan, the culture of the castle town and its surrounding countryside was homogeneous and there was no need for the town to defend itself against an alien culture.

As the centuries went by, Japan's cities grew and expanded, and the three great cities of Edo, Kyoto, and Osaka developed very different characters. In the eighteenth century there was much debate about their comparative characteristics and about improvement of the cities. Most argued that Edo was the city of the samurai elite and political leadership; Kyoto was the city of the aristocracy and the handicraft industries, and Osaka was the merchant's city and economic center of the country. Indeed, until about the middle of the nineteenth century, the population of men was greater in Edo than that of women. Kyoto, moreover, had been producing fine handicrafts since its height as the capital in the Heian period which continued to pass into the hands of the upper strata of society throughout the country. The Kyoto industries were sustained by the aesthetic tastes cultivated by the idle court nobility. And Osaka, with its advantageous location on the edge of the Inland Sea, became an immense depot where all kinds of goods, including farm produce from the highly developed agricultural areas along the coast of the Inland Sea were delivered and distributed to the rest of the country.

By this time, Japan was fast losing the closed and unified quality Gyōki had depicted it as having centuries earlier. It was no longer a country with a single nucleus located at Kyoto, but a multipolar nation with nuclei not only at these three major cities, but at each local castle town as well. Exchange with other countries gradually increased, and people became aware that the world around Japan was not inhabited by monstrous human beings and demons. By the beginning of the eighteenth century, Japan's leaders had obtained Blaeu's map of the world through the Dutch at Nagasaki, and the Confucian scholar-official Arai Hakuseki (1657-1725) had compiled a major work on world geography called the *Sairan igen* (Accounts of Foreign Languages and Western Geography). In 1709, a work compiling information about the world from Chinese books on Western geography was published by Nishikawa Jōken (1648-1724) entitled *Kai tsūshō kō* (A Study of Transport and Commerce in China and the West). It was well known, at least among educated people, that Japan was just one small realm within an immense world. They also knew that the world outside was divided into many states each of which had a culture different from that of Japan.

With the spread of this wider awareness of the world, a movement aimed at mapping a more accurate image of Japan emerged. What was to be the shape of the country that would replace

The 48 teams of fire brigades in Edo turn out for the traditional New Year's Day parade.

Gyōki's map? Various efforts began toward creating a new map of Japan. The first to be completed was a map of the Japanese archipelago by Nagakubo Sekisui (1717-1801) in 1779. This was published and widely distributed, and the outlines of the country were much closer to reality. With the appearance of this map, the awareness of Japan as part of the larger world became well established. Then in 1792, Shiba Kōkan (1747-1818) provided a global map, which along with his celestial map, gave people a very specific image of Japan's place in the world.

Meanwhile, the distinctive urban cultures of Edo, Osaka and Kyoto grew and flourished. The feudal system became the accepted norm for all citizens, and during the period of peace overlapping three centuries, the life of the townspeople became very settled. It seemed as if the peace would go on forever and that there was nothing that could rock the immovable feudal system that had been established. Japan was as yet a closed system.

The culture that developed in this sheltered world took on an increasingly popular character. The cultural leaders who were responsible for the flowering of popular culture came from many different classes. The closed social order produced a hothouse effect, causing the subdivision and progressive specialization of cultural traditions. The trend was sustained by the wealthy citizens of the cities, who were gradually growing into a new leisure class, and the well-to-do samurai. During the prolonged peace, the samurai began to turn their passions away from military exploits to cultural pursuits. Novelists, painters, art collectors, and devotees of this or that art or discipline began to emerge out of their ranks. Leaders in culture and the arts appeared, too, from among the wealthy townspeople. Eventually the leaders of culture rose above the categories of social class and position to exchange ideas and, in some cases, to form groups. Their activities were promoted and facilitated by the growth of the well-informed and economically solid urban townspeople.

Urban life in Japan from the eighteenth to the nineteenth century differed little from what it has been in very recent times. A variety of value systems emerged and existed side by side among the townspeople. The majority were realistic and positive in outlook, and all were intensive and differentiated by very fine sensibilities. Diversity and refinement within the bounds of tradition flourished because of a period without precedent in world history, of peace lasting approximately three hundred years and of social stability maintained by isolation from direct contact with other cultures.

Illustrated Works

15th Century

Buddhism in Japan underwent a major reformation in the thirteenth century at the hands of two priests, Hōnen (1133-1212) and Shinran (1173-1263). Hōnen believed that the world had entered the corrupt age of the "latter day of the (*dharma*) law," and taught that all man could do was to repent his own depravity and pray to the Amida Buddha for salvation. This was a fundamentally different approach to the religion that had until then been chiefly the preserve of the literate classes—the court, aristocracy and bureaucracy— where it was understood mainly in intellectual terms. Hōnen taught that even without a literal under-standing of the sutras, man could be saved simply through *nembutsu* or the recitation of Amida's name. According to his belief, the Buddha was a transcendental being different from man, but through prayer, the Buddha would cast down the saving light upon human beings.

Shinran carried these teachings even further. He believed that the gap as well as the conflict between the Buddha and man lay within man's mind. If man would of his own volition repent his sins and chant the *nembutsu*, Shinran taught, his heart would become one with the heart of the Buddha, and he could be assured of salvation after death. He stressed that the Buddha and man did not exist in different worlds; that the Buddha was present within in the individual.

The teachings of these two great reformers gained a wide following among the general populace. Hōnen and Shinran introduced a new principle of religious grouping that transcended social class, bringing into being communities with extremely strong bonds of religious fellowship. These are the Jōdo Shin and Jōdo sects, which even today are important religious bodies in Japan. These schools, unlike any others in the history of Japanese religion, sought the realization of a religious kingdom, and they clashed frequently with political authorities. From the fifteenth century onward, however, the various schools of Buddhism became recognized parts of the establishment.

Coincidental with this movement through which the concept of the oneness of man and the Buddha was becoming widespread, was the introduction of Zen from China. Zen Buddhism was brought to Japan by the priests Yōsai (also known as Eisai; 1141-1215) and Dōgen (1200-1253) at the same time that Hōnen and Shinran were active. Zen required strict observance of precepts as well as rigorous self-imposed discipline and training. Training consisted most importantly of meditation. The Buddhahood within oneself could not be discovered through ritual acts such as burning incense, prayer to the Buddha, or reading of the sutras; it depended, above all, on the act of simply sitting in meditation.

For the common people, for whom work meant survival, a religious discipline that required mainly meditation was hardly feasible. And Zen, unlike the Jōdo Shin and Jōdo sects, made no attempt to appeal to the masses. Still, like Jōdo Shin, Zen made the reality of human existence its starting point, and this appealed to the warrior class, whose lives were played out in the no-man's-land between life and death. Zen was also the latest import from Japan's mentor, China, and brought back directly by Yōsai and Dōgen, who represented the vanguard of the intellectual elite. Thus Zen grew and spread in Japan as the Buddhism of the warrior class. Many Zen temples were built in Kyoto, particularly after the new shogunal government returned there in the fourteenth century. It was the Zen clergy who took the lead in the transplantation of Sung and Ming culture from China.

Zen emphasized solitary training and individual meditation. Man should live within the embrace of nature, and in nature he must first of all discover himself. Dōgen established his base of training and discipline at Eiheiji, far north of Kyoto in the mountains of the Hokuriku district. There might be Zen temples in the city, but he believed that it was necessary to live in intimate contact with nature in a completely natural landscape. This is part of the reason that the Zen temples of Kyoto were all located on the outskirts of the city.

The Zen temple garden, moreover, had to be a place encapsulating the natural landscape where man could discover his own being through the Buddha as manifest in nature. The landscape as seen after rising from deep meditation was changeless in shape and form. Indeed, through meditation, man encountered nature anew, in the realization that it was an expression of the absolute being which is called Buddha.

This conception of nature was the reason that *suiboku* painting, introduced by Japanese priests who had studied Zen in China, became the central form of art of the time. *Suiboku* paintings are monochromatic works executed in *sumi* ink, usually with a vast landscape of mountains and streams. Man, if he is present at all, appears only as an extremely tiny figure. Many have calligraphic inscriptions in an upper corner, usually added by a person other than the painter, providing an interpretation of the painting in poetic form. These poems are considered as being as important as, and an integral part of the painting itself.

The basic principle of Chinese literati taste was the equivalence of poetry, calligraphy and painting, and the capacity to fuse all these three genre was the hallmark of the most distinguished men of letters. The ability to make three such divergent forms of expression converge meant that man had to be versatile enough to move from one to the other freely, rather like wandering in a dream or fantasy. Devotion to the literati arts, in fact, involved absorption in the world of dream and illusion. Immersed in the beauties of poetry, or calligraphy or painting, one became completely a part of the world of dream and illusion. He might revert to the world of reality now and then, but in the process of repeated comings and goings, the line between the two would grow hardly distinguishable.

The people who constantly moved back and forth between reality and illusion were unconventional, eccentric figures who appeared to ordinary people to be somewhat mad. They were examples of the ultimate freedom of the human being, equivalent to a kind of primeval man. Here, man is, like the mountains and streams, part of the landscape itself. Just as the landscape alters with the turning of each season, man himself changes with shifts in mood and frame of mind. From the point of view of people who are constantly under the control of outside forces, this appeared to be "madness." One of the most notable of mad eccentrics was Ikkyū Sōjun (1394-1481). Ikkyū called himself Kyōun, or "crazy cloud," in other words, nature in a mad ecstacy. Just as nature is everywhere unchanging existence, Ikkyū was unalterably human, but when such a human being behaved in the same manner as nature, the world thought him mad. Ikkyū couched his unconventional behavior in a cutting wit and parody, taking a consistently critical stand against the Zen priests who resided in grand temples, posed as the cultural elite in their association with upper-stratum intellectuals, and even acted as consultants to high-ranking government figures.

Expression of the archetype of the madman obsessed with nature and the world of illusion was brought to the performing arts by Zeami (1363-1443), playwright, critic, and founder of the Noh drama. These plays focused on death, looking at man both in the world of the living and the world of the dead. In this life, the human being is surrounded with all kinds of people, but once he dies, he passes into the realm of the dead and a world of total solitude. What happens in the after-life is linked to life before death according to the Buddhist precept of cause and effect. Man lives only once, and once he dies that sole human existence is absorbed into the eternity of the world of the dead.

Zeami expressed the concept of free interplay between illusion and reality by the word *yūgen*. *Yūgen* denoted a gentle grace, and in dramatic or musical expression, a beauty of serenity and quietude. These qualities, in fact, were those emphasized in the canons of the literary arts of the medieval period, particularly *waka* poetry. This poetic genre was a symbolic short-verse form, and the method of expressing this symbolism was described as *yūgen*. Zeami merely carried that method of expression to the level of dramatic performance.

Zeami transformed the arts of Noh, which up until that time had been performed in the shrines as part of rituals for the entertainment of the gods, into the form of dramatic plays intended for human audiences. Zeami spoke often of what he called *hana* (flower), by which he meant the impression of beauty and vividness felt by those watching a play. If the actors had mastered the spirit of *yūgen*, those watching would see their performance with a freshness and keenness described as the "flower."

Noh became very popular not only among the elite but among the people at large. It became a new form of performing art in the cities, and in time it was taken up by amateurs as well. Side-by-side with the Noh, moreover, arose a form of comedy called Kyōgen, which satirized and poked fun at the realities of contemporary society. In the new performing arts of the fifteenth century, the symbolism of the Noh and the realism of Kyōgen were an indivisible pair.

Portraits

Ashikaga Yoshimitsu

Henry the Navigator

Sesshū Tōyō

Ashikaga Yoshimitsu (1358-1408) —
The third Ashikaga shogun. Yoshimitsu
succeeded his father in 1368 at the age of
ten. A brilliant leader, he ended an
imperial succession dispute between the
split northern and southern courts
(creating a single court again) and con-
solidated his position by defeating military rivals, bringing order to much of
Japan. He also brought back Kyoto's
glory as a cultural center by ignoring the
conservative aristocracy and seeking out
artists from among the common people.
His generous patronage of the arts
spawned a cultural renaissance that
received inspiration from his renewal of
ties with China. He retired to Kinkakuji,
the temple of the golden pavilion, which
he had built in the hills north of Kyoto.

Zeami (1363-1443) —
Thespian and playwright who perfected
Noh drama. Zeami was an eleven-year-
old child-actor in his father's theatrical
troupe when his boyish genius, grace
and good looks attracted the attention of
the Shogun Ashikaga Yoshimitsu. Zeami
joined Yoshimitsu's highly artistic Kyoto
court where he refined Noh, then
scorned as *sarugaku* or mere mimicry,
into a theatrical art. He wrote his own
plays as well as rewriting most of the
Noh plays that existed at the time. The
transmission of his secret acting techniques, hidden during a dispute between
members of the troupe that survived
him, were only rediscovered in the early
1900s and speak of *hana* (flower) meaning a superb actor and *yūgen* (subtle
beauty), a fine performance or play. Like
all great Japanese artists, Zeami thought
of art—particularly the theatrical art—as
the way (*michi*) to human perfection.

See pp.30-31

Ikkyū Sōjun (1394-1481) —
Eccentric Zen Buddhist monk said to
have been the illegitimate son of an
emperor and a low-born noblewoman.
He delighted in shocking people out of
their worldly complacency using an idiosyncratic style of Zen—often doing
things in exaggerated or topsy-turvy
manner to illustrate the hypocrisy they
tried to hide. He spent years in a small
mountain temple from where he attacked the excesses and corruption of Kyoto's
Zen temples. Nevertheless, he had ties
with the nouveau riche merchant class.
He was known for his poetry and calligraphy, and associated with leading
cultural figures. In 1474, at age 81, he
became the abbot of Daitokuji after it
burned down, helping to rebuild it
physically and spiritually. Unconventional to the end, he had a much talked-
about love affair with a blind singer late
in his life.

See pp.32-33

Sesshū Tōyō (1420-1506) —
The first Japanese painter to give bor-
rowed Chinese techniques an original
Japanese flavor. Born in the countryside
in western Japan, Sesshū at a young age
went to Kyoto where he became a Buddhist monk and studied painting under a
renowned master. Sesshū left the then
politically unstable Kyoto, however, for
Yamaguchi far west of his birthplace. He
spent two years travelling in Ming China
under the munificence of his Yamaguchi
patrons, returning in 1469. His style fea-
tures dynamic brushwork and structural
composition and, though he painted
portraits and other figure subjects, he is
best known for his architectonic land-

scapes. He was the first to use actual
sites in Japan as the subjects of his
works rather than imaginery, idealized
Chinese-style scenes.

See pp.34-35

Hosokawa Katsumoto (1430-1473) —
Military governor who also served three
terms as shogunal deputy. Katsumoto's
first term as shogunal deputy began
when he was fifteen, and he eventually
became one of two de facto leaders of
the shogunate. A shogunal succession
dispute in the Ashikaga family, with
Katsumoto and another warrior family
on opposing sides led to the Onin War
(1467-77), during which Katsumoto's
armies participated in the devastation of
Kyoto. Earlier, in 1450, Katsumoto, who
was an avid Zen practitioner, built
Ryoanji Temple in the northwest part of
Kyoto. The temple exists today though it
is much smaller, and it is known for its
"dry landscape" style rock garden which
is composed of fifteen stones surrounded
by a bed of white sand.

See p.40

Ashikaga Yoshimasa (1435-1490) —
Yoshimitsu's grandson and the eighth
Ashikaga shogun. A disinterested
military man—perhaps because he
inherited power at age seven and had
grown up pampered and effete—
Yoshimasa was a failure as shogun and
even his retirement only helped preci-
pitate the Onin War. Undaunted, he was
a patron of the arts on a par with, if not
the better of, his grandfather, establishing a cultural enclave in the hills east of
Kyoto. While his grandfather's court
brought Noh drama to its peak, Yoshimasa's court found its specialty in linked
verse. In his eastern Kyoto hideaway,

Hosokawa Katsumoto

Ashikaga Yoshimasa

Da Vinci, Leonardo

Michelangelo, Buonarroti

Yoshimasa built a retreat that later became Ginkakuji, the silver pavilion. He dreamed of covering it with silver leaf to further the contrast with Yoshimitsu's Kinkakuji, the golden pavilion, but died before he could carry out his plans.

Kanō Motonobu (1476-1559) ——————
The genius credited with unifying Chinese and indigenous painting traditions. The son of the founder of the Kanō school of painting, Motonobu was at home in a variety of techniques which he used according to patrons' requests. He enjoyed, moreover, patronage from every level of social status and thus shows a chameleon-like virtuosity in his work. A true eclectic, he merged all the styles he had studied and learned into his own style, going so far as to symbolically seal the achievement by marrying the daughter of Tosa Mitsunobu of the rival Tosa school. His works, known for their dramatic simplicity, are best represented by his sliding screen doors. Some of his screens were even sent to China. See pp.36-37

Tosa Mitsunobu (1480-1522) ——————
The last great scroll painting artist and the reviver of the Tosa school of painting. The Tosa school preserved the indigenous style of painting even when it went out of favor in a period of heavily Chinese-influenced art, though their works were of little distinction. Mitsunobu brought back a measure of respect to this Japanese style and to his school—the official artists of the imperial court (as opposed to the shogunal artists, the Kanō school)—through such works as the *Legends of Kiyomizu Temple* and the *Legends of Seiryō Temple*.
See pp.38-39

Henry the Navigator (1394-1460)
Sponsors exploration of Africa

Gutenberg, Johann (1398-1468)
Inventor of movable type

Bellini, Giovanni (1430-1516)
Italian painter

Botticelli, Sandro (1444/5-1510)
Italian painter

Columbus, Christopher (1446 or 1451-1506)
Explorer of the New World

Lorenzo de' Medici (1449-1492)
Renaissance ruler

Bosch, Hieronymus (1450-1516)
Dutch painter

Da Vinci, Leonardo (1452-1519)
Renaissance artist and
Scientific genius

Copernicus, Nicolaus (1473-1543)
Polish scientist

Michelangelo, Buonarroti (1475-1564)
Italian painter, sculptor, architect

Luther, Martin (1483-1546)
German reformation leader

Raphael (1483-1520)
Italian painter

Rabelais, François (1495-1553)
French writer

Holbein, Hans (the Younger) (1497-1543)
German painter

花伝第六花修云

In Zeami's masterpiece, *Izutsu* (The Well Curb), the ghost of a poet's wife dances in her husband's clothes. 31

Ikkyū Sōjun (1394-1481)

32   Portrait of the Zen priest Ikkyū who rebuilt Daitokuji Temple in Kyoto by raising funds from rich merchants in Sakai

An example of Ikkyū's calligraphy, famous for its radically expressive form: this ideograph means *"shū"* or "everything."

Sesshū Tōyō (1420-1506)

34 Winter Landscape by Sesshū, painted during his sojourn in Ming China

36   Motonobu's *Birds and Flowers of the Four Seasons*, painted on sliding doors of Daisen-in Temple in Kyoto.   The original

has remained in storage since it was vandalized, but the copy exhibited here is still 110 years old.

Mitsunobu's *Origin and History of Jokoji Temple* vividly portrays the court lifestyle of the 13th century. *39*

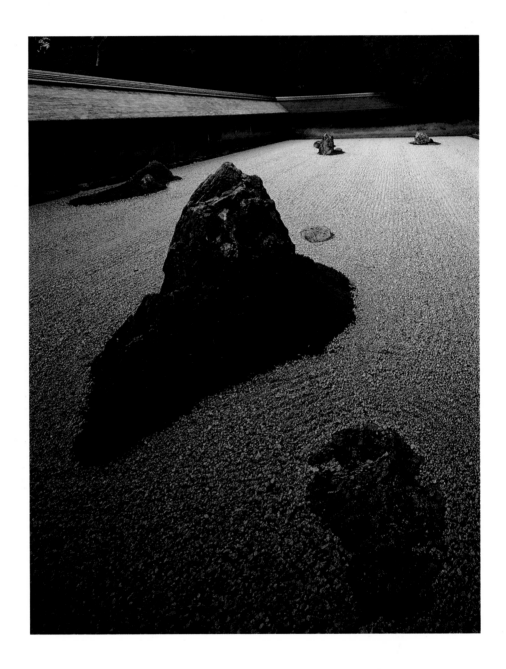

The Zen-style garden of Ryoanji Temple, built by Hosokawa Katsumoto in 1450 in Kyoto

16th Century

In the sixteenth century a new culture began to bud in Edo in the eastern part of the country, taking its place next to the classical culture of Kyoto which had been the sole metropolis in the country since the eighth century. As the new order began to flower, the old cultural order that had matured under the leadership of the aristocracy was eventually completely overshadowed. It was an epochal time of cultural revolution. The roots of almost all the elements of so-called traditional culture that are alive in Japan today, in fact, go back to this period.

After centuries of internal strife, the country was finally unified by Oda Nobunaga, Toyotomi Hideyoshi, and Tokugawa Ieyasu, who marshalled unchallengeable military and economic power to forge the local hegemonies of the provincial warlords into a centralized feudal structure. Nobunaga, who began the process of unifying the country, set up his base of operations in Azuchi, not far from Kyoto, and around the huge castle he built there a new city took shape. Hideyoshi, his successor, completed the unification of Japan, and established his headquarters first in Kyoto and then in Osaka, where he built huge castles. At the same time, in Kyoto he instituted many urban planning improvements and in Osaka initiated a plan for new development of the city. Ieyasu, who cemented the grip of shogunal rule over the country, established his court at Edo, creating the bipolar structure of political and spiritual leadership that prevailed in Japan throughout the subsequent two-hundred and fifty years.

The established pattern of rule in Japan, modeled after that of China, was based on a structure of power with the emperor at the top and controlled and administered by the aristocracy and the bureaucracy. The shoguns who held the reins of government from the twelfth century to the end of the Sengoku period had remained relatively faithful to this traditional pattern of government. The three great leaders of sixteenth century Japan, however, were men of rural origins from the central part of the island of Honshū in the vicinity of present-day Nagoya. They adopted a completely new pattern of rule based on agrarian principles. They introduced elements from Japan's communal society centering on wet-rice agriculture, one of the most important of which was the *yoriai*, a form of council. They did not abolish the traditional bureaucracy, with the emperor at its apex, but preserved it as a hierarchy of prestige, creating alongside it the military and political organization that held real power. This organization was based on principles that governed agrarian communal groups and it was this body that was responsible for creating the feudal society of the next three-hundred years.

Their roots in the countryside, the new leaders were above all realistic, often outright despotic, and they expressed their realism through extravagant displays of economic power. The interiors of their immense castles and palaces were covered with gilt and every shining surface was ornamented with paintings in gorgeous, dazzling color. The lavishly decorated interiors and huge architectural spaces they created were the equivalent of the splendid Baroque palaces built by the absolute monarchs of Europe. Hideyoshi's famous palace, Jurakudai, was perhaps the most magnificent. The complex, no longer extant today, measured 440 meters east to west and 770 meters north to south, an immense building combining private and administrative quarters surrounded completely by a moat. The interior of every room was decorated with gilt and colorful paintings. Construction of such edifices, as well as Hideyoshi's rebuilding and development projects throughout Kyoto brought unprecedented prosperity to the artisans and merchants of the city. Most of the successful handicraft establishments that still do business today, in fact, trace their beginnings to this early period.

Within the Jurakudai palace there were numerous rooms as well as detached pavilions specially designed for performance of the tea ceremony. Among them were tea houses built by individual *daimyō* who were Hideyoshi's vassals. They were modeled after farm cottages or mountain hermitages, but constructed in the most refined taste and with the most carefully selected materials. Having risen to the position of supreme power and authority, Hideyoshi and his followers lived out their days in grandeur and palatial splendor. These tea huts, scattered among gilt-covered, brightly painted halls, provided plain, unpretentious spaces where men who had grown up in far humbler surroundings could seek refuge and relaxation.

The uses of tea had been introduced to Japan by the Zen priest Yōsai in the thirteenth century, and tea plantations became widespread in the western part of Japan. In time, tea became the focus of connoisseurship, and salons emerged at which people gathered to share the pleasures of tea drinking. After the beginning of the fourteenth century, in particular, a wide variety of gatherings centering on the drinking of tea were held among members of the warrior elite, and in the fifteenth century tea parties became a popular pastime of both high-ranking samurai as well as court nobles. These parties, exemplary of the epicureanism of urban society of the time, were generally held in spacious halls that accommodated fifty to one hundred guests. They began with a contest in which the guests sampled several varieties of tea and competed to identify the name and origin of each variety. Prizes were awarded for the most skillful taster, and the guests subsequently treated to a banquet with plentiful food and drink.

Toward the end of the fifteenth century, a man named Murata Jukō (1423-1502) had originated a completely different approach to tea drinking in which a few friends met in small, sparsely adorned rooms. This new style, focused simply on the drinking of tea, gradually became very popular, especially among the wealthy merchants of Sakai, a port and commercial center near Osaka then prospering from the trade with China, as well as of Kyoto and Nara. The merchants of the sixteenth century enjoyed immense wealth and power, and some came to the realization that by occasionally removing themselves to simpler, humbler surroundings, they could discover a new dimension of themselves. Their small tea gatherings served as a vehicle for cultivating communal bonds based on shared cultural values. The utensils they used in serving tea, moreover, were subtle symbols of their wealth. The most highly prized were tea bowls and tea jars imported from China, which were bought and sold for high prices. Jesuit priests who came to Japan at this time were amazed to find that tea ceremony utensils were valued just as highly by the Japanese elite as were fine jewels by European aristocrats. They were quick to realize that to gain the respect of the upper strata of society in Japan and a hearing for their religion, it behooved them to be conversant in the tea ceremony.

The attractions of tea ceremony in the new style were not lost on the warrior leaders who grasped actual power. They recognized its value as a means of displaying their wealth as well as of establishing ties with cultural groups in the cities. They became enthusiastic practitioners of the tea ceremony as well as collectors of the most prized of tea ceremony utensils. Hideyoshi, who rose to power from the humble status of foot soldier, astutely followed their example. Like all the rest, his devotion to tea was in part the result of his urge to flaunt his wealth and power. In 1582 he had a tea room built that was completely covered with gold leaf and equipped it with a full set of utensils made of gold. In 1587 he arranged a grand outdoor tea party at the Kitano Shrine in Kyoto at which some 800 hosts built temporary tea huts to serve the thousands of guests invited to attend.

The leader of the tea ceremony in the sixteenth century was Sen no Rikyū (1522-91), a man of merchant background in Sakai. He carried on the tradition of tea served in simple, humble surroundings that had started with Murata Jukō, and became the authority on good taste in tea utensils, establishing many of the norms of the tea ceremony including the shape of many tea bowls and correct conduct and etiquette for attendance at tea ceremonies. Rikyū is responsible for the stylization of the tea ceremony as well as for the introduction of the fundamental concept of tea as the search for the self, reflecting the influence of Zen discipline and meditation. He considered the ultimate tea ceremony a private, contemplative occasion revolving around an individual's conversations with himself. In this he sharply clashed with Hideyoshi, who had a preference for the ostentatious and pretentious. Although Rikyū served as Hideyoshi's adviser in matters of tea for many years, the rift between them deepened and in 1591 Hideyoshi ordered Rikyū to commit *seppuku*.

Meanwhile, the cities grew and prospered through the ambitious and extravagant projects of the men in power. A substantial body of wealthy citizens became established in the cities, and gradually they began to create a new system of values in a world removed from that of the centers of power. In this process they took as their standard the culture of the Heian court at its height around the eleventh century, and sought a revival of its ancient glories. The culture of the court of the eleventh century had been a Baroque-like world revolving around aestheticism. All events and ceremonies, as well as literature and even matters of love were highly stylized and conducted with elaborate melodrama. The new aesthetic ideal of the sixteenth-century townspeople was the revival of the literary images of the Heian age and the incorporation of those images into painting and other forms of artistic expression. In the process they produced fresh, original designs that remain alive and popular today, transcending both time and tradition.

People in all walks of life in the sixteenth century reveled in the new urban culture. They enjoyed theatrical performances of popularized forms of Noh and Kyōgen and relished the intoxicating excitement afforded by shrine festivals. In spring they sang and drank to the exquisite beauty of the cherry blossoms and in autumn went on picnics to enjoy the brilliant colors of the maple trees. These and other pleasures that are a part of popular urban life even today can be traced to this century of fresh beginnings.

Portraits

Sen no Rikyū

Elizabeth I

Oda Nobunaga

Sen no Rikyū (1522-1591) ————
Tea ceremony master who became the arbiter of good taste during a time of cultural and artistic experimentation in Japan. The son of a fish merchant, Rikyū studied several types of tea ceremony before becoming the official tea ceremony performer for Oda Nobunaga and, later, Toyotomi Hideyoshi. Rikyū's love of the simple and restrained put a curb on the gaudy excesses of the times. He reduced the size of the tea ceremony house (*chashitsu*) to two or even just one and a half tatami mats, and introduced flower holders made of bamboo, rough tea bowls and simple iron kettles. Rikyū fell suddenly out of favor with Hideyoshi—the reason is still being debated—and he was forced to commit suicide.
See pp.46-47

Oda Nobunaga (1534-1582) ————
Samurai warlord, the first of the "three great unifiers of Japan." Nicknamed the "great idiot" for his strange behavior at his father's funeral, Nobunaga skillfully put down disorder in his inherited lands and set out to control all of Japan. Absolutely ruthless in battle, Nobunaga was also a lavish and eager supporter of the arts. He indulged a personal curiosity in Christianity by allowing Christians to practice their religion in Japan. He was attacked in a temple in Kyoto by one of his own vassals and died a samurai death under his own hand.

Toyotomi Hideyoshi (1536-1598) ————
Samurai warlord, the second of the "three great unifiers of Japan." Hideyoshi was the son of a foot soldier, but by 1558 had attracted the attention of Nobunaga, whom he served. After Nobunaga's death, he seized power, strengthening

his position by continuing Nobunaga's strong, innovative policies: redistributing land to favor loyal vassals and weaken provincial lords, ordering land surveys, outlawing private ownership of swords, and taking a census that defined social status. Like Nobunaga, he patronized the arts, but he outlawed Christianity in 1587.

Hasegawa Tōhaku (1539-1610) ————
The founder of the Hasegawa school of painting, known for his ink paintings of monkeys and gibbons done in the Zen style. Tōhaku was adopted by a family of dyers in what is now Ishikawa prefecture. A student of the Kanō school of painting, he later claimed to be Sesshū's artistic descendant, but lost a legal dispute (with rival Unkoku Tōgan) over the right to publicly say so. The oldest extant painting with Tōhaku's signature dates to 1589. Many of the works thought to be his are recent attributions which came about after much study and debate.
See pp.48-49

Kanō Eitoku (1543-1590) ————
Motonobu's grandson and the most sought-after artist of his day. Eitoku received his initial instruction from his grandfather, but it was his own dramatic style of color-and-gold screen and wall paintings that brought him fame and influenced painters in succeeding years. Many of his works were destroyed, sometimes just after completion, by the constant warfare between military families that characterized the turbulent age. Paintings that are verifiably his display simplified motifs on a large, almost theatrical scales, broad, rough, lively brushstrokes, and vibrant colors that contrast vividly with the gold leaf background.

See pp.50-51

Hon'ami Kōetsu (1558-1637) ————
Versatile artist of talent, equally at home with calligraphy, pottery and lacquer and metal design. Kōetsu, the son of a sword expert, did not become well-known until the death of his father in 1603. His first important work was the production and publication of some books of illustrated Noh plays and selections from classical literature. Kōetsu's calligraphy won him praise as one of the "Three Brushes" of the era. In 1615, he retired to Takagamine, northwest of Kyoto, to a tract of land granted him by Ieyasu. There he gathered about him a community of artists and the Rimpa style of painting, craft and design was developed under his direction.
See pp.52-55

Kobori Enshū (1579-1647) ————
Tea ceremony master of many talents. The son of the commissioner of public works in Ōmi province (now Shiga prefecture), Enshū became an architect like his father, allegedly designing some of the finest gardens in Kyoto. But at an early age he studied tea ceremony under a disciple of Rikyū's and eventually served as a tea adviser to Shogun Tokugawa Ieyasu. Known as a man of impeccable taste, Enshū had such an influence on the techniques and materials used in producing tea wares that after his death seven types of pottery became associated with his name. He was also a calligrapher and poet, and is said to have practiced flower arrangement as well.
See pp.60-61

Hayashi Razan (1583-1657) ————
Scholar, educator and historian. Born to

Shakespeare, William

Galilei, Galileo

Hayashi Razan

Toyotomi Hideyoshi

a declining samurai family, Razan was adopted by a rice dealer. He studied Zen at a Kyoto temple but, refusing to take the tonsure, began studying Neo-Confucianism. Erudite and energetic, Razan attracted the attention of the shogunate, which brought him into official government service, thus establishing Neo-Confucianism as a semiofficial orthodoxy. Razan was a noted ideologue and propagandist—he strongly supported the anti-Christian movement. He was rewarded with land and money to start a school and his family remained official advisors for several generations.

Miyamoto Musashi (1584-1645) ——
Master swordsman, painter and calligrapher known for his two-sword style of fighting and for his ink paintings. A *rōnin*, a masterless samurai, Musashi engaged in and won more than sixty sword fights while traveling around Japan. Musashi later became a swordsmanship instructor for a military family on the island of Kyushu in southern Japan and helped the government put down the Shimabara rebellion of 1637. His book on swordsmanship, *The Book of Five Rings*, is considered a martial classic. A highly esteemed painter, Musashi is known for his ink paintings of eagles, shrike and Buddhist figures. His bold and incisive brushwork reveals the influence of his Zen training.
See pp.62-63

Sakaida Kakiemon (1596-1666) ——
Ceramic artist who originated the polychrome overglaze enameled porcelain. Information is scarce about Kakiemon, but tradition has it that, using overglaze pigments imported from China, he made Japan's first polychrome porcelains at his

family's Nangawara kiln in 1643. Thirty years later he was being imitated by Japanese artists and by the turn of the century, by Chinese artists, and his influence moved to Europe as well. The family line continues to this day.
See p.64

Izumo no Okuni (?-early 1600s) ——
Acknowledged "originator" of Kabuki drama. Okuni's background is obscure, but popular accounts hold that she was a former attendant of Izumo Shrine, a major Shinto center, and later became the leader of a troupe of female dancers in Kyoto. Okuni's troupe performed the *nembutsu* dance, a dance with religious ties which is still done today. Her troupe won popular acclaim in 1603, the date regarded as the beginning of Kabuki. Okuni also allegedly appeared as a male in some skits of a bawdy nature, in part leading to an eventual ban on female Kabuki performers.
See pp.56-57

Tawaraya Sōtatsu (?-1643?) ——
Artist and one of the founders of the Rimpa style of painting. Little is known of Sōtatsu's personal life, though it is believed he came from merchant stock (possibly a family of fan makers). Some "poem cards" Sōtatsu did feature Hon'ami Kōetsu's calligraphy of five-line tanka poems written over his paintings of flowers, grass and animals. Sōtatsu attempted to revive traditional Yamato painting done in color with gold and silver backgrounds on screens, scrolls, fans, writing paper and album leaves. Unlike his predecessors, however, Sōtatsu chose his themes from the cultural past of Japan, and not China.
See pp.58-59

Palladio, Andrea (1508-1580)
Italian architect

Ronsard, Pierre de (1524-1585)
French poet

Brueghel, Pieter (the Elder) (1525-1569)
Dutch painter

Montaigne, Michel de (1533-1592)
French author

Elizabeth I (1533-1603)
English ruler

El Greco (1541-1614)
Spanish painter

Cervantes, Miguel de (1547-1616)
Spanish writer

Bacon, Francis (1561-1626)
English philosopher

Shakespeare, William (1564-1616)
English dramatist and poet

Galilei, Galileo (1564-1642)
Italian scientist

Rubens, Peter Paul (1577-1640)
Flemish painter

Descartes, René (1596-1650)
French philosopher

Van Dyck, Anthony (1599-1641)
Flemish painter

Velázquez, Diego (1599-1660)
Spanish painter

46 Rikyū, ordered to commit hara-kiri, gave his tea scoop (right) as a keepsake to his disciple Oribe who named it "tears."

48   The lavish gold leaf background on this painting of a maple tree by Tōhaku reflects the changing trend of art from simplicity

o extravagance under Toyotomi Hideyoshi, a foot soldier who sought to put his humble origins behind him.

Kano Eitoku (1543-1590)

A scene of Kyoto by Eitoku shows its citizens enjoying the revival of the famous Gion Festival following the Onin civil war.

An autumn poem in calligraphy by Kōetsu written over a painting attributed to Tawaraya Sōtatsu.

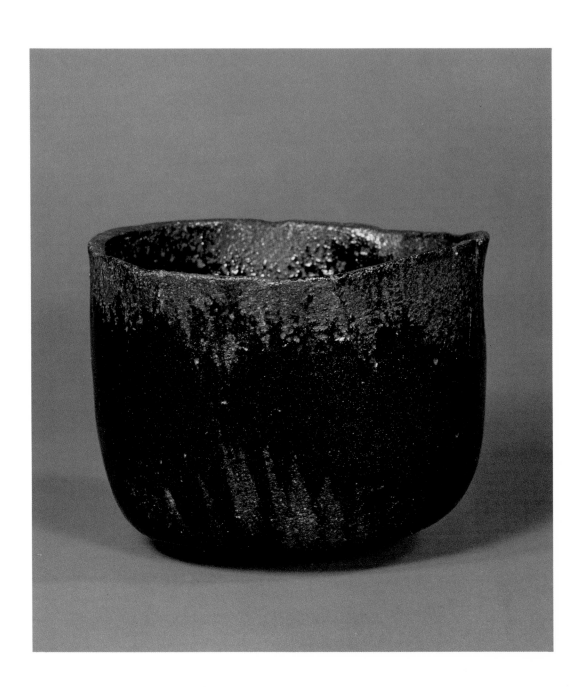

This famous hand-molded black *raku* tea bowl by Kōetsu is named *Amagumo* (Rain Cloud) after its dripping glaze.   *53*

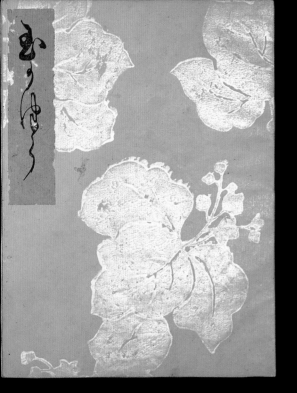

Kōetsu's versatility led him to collaborate with the wealthy businessman Suminokura Soan in designing and publishing.

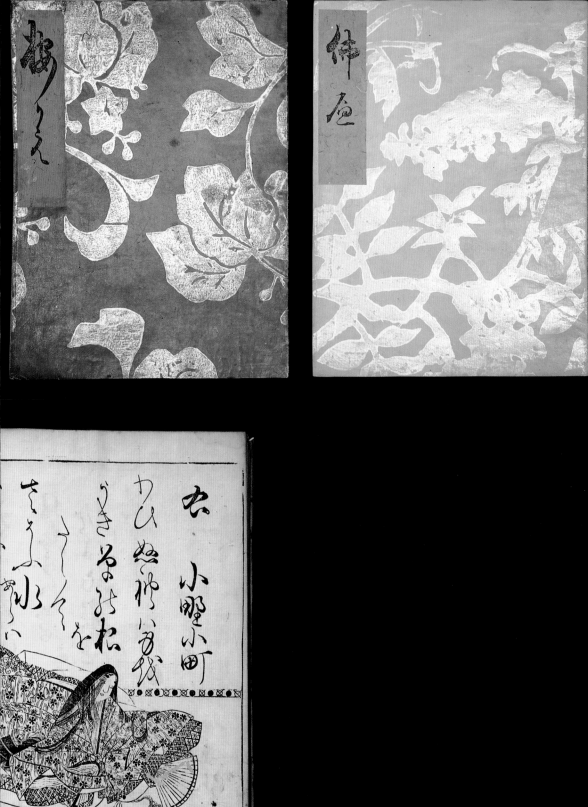

六　小野小町

わひぬれは身をうき草の
ねをたえてさそふ水あ
らはいなむとそおも
ふ

The star performer on stage in this Kabuki scene is Okuni, the originator of Kabuki drama.

This folk dance performed in the villages of Niigata prefecture is one of a few that retain the style of Okuni today.

58 A screen painting of the famous scenic spot, Matsushima, by Sōtatsu who started a new tradition of realistic representation.

Kobori Enshū (1579-1647)

It took Enshū five years to create this dry landscape garden at Konchi-in, part of Nanzenji Temple in Kyoto. He completed it in 16

Musashi's irony is depicted in the worm in mid-branch whose fate hangs on the whim of the shrike above.

The simple straw sash Musashi always wore symbolizes his emphasis on the fundamentals in life.

Sakaida Kakiemon (1596-1666)

This jar is by Kakiemon, believed to be the first Japanese creator of polychrome porcelain.

17th Century

Events of the seventeenth century are dominated by the construction of the city of Edo, where Tokugawa Ieyasu established his new base of power following the death of Hideyoshi, and by the creation of the system of control by which the numerous domains were welded into a unified state. The institutions of feudal society that functioned with little change for almost three centuries until the middle of the nineteenth century were solidified in the early decades of the century. The new regime preserved the traditional court ranks centering on the emperor as a hierarchy of prestige, while creating in Edo a separate hierarchy of political authority based on the national hegemony of the Tokugawa clan. The political system thus created, the shogunate, functioned on the principle of agrarian communal society. There were few statutory laws and government was conducted empirically, largely on the basis of precedent and practice. Laws and ordinances, put in effect for an unspecified period of time, were publicized in the form of edicts posted throughout the country.

Sovereignty of the country was divided among numerous *daimyō* or feudal lords whose domains were virtually autonomous fiefs, each comprising a distinct political, military, economic, as well as cultural realm. Some domains issued locally circulating currency. The *daimyō* were subject to the shogun, the supreme military dictator of the country and head of the Tokugawa clan, and to the military administration or *bakufu*. The headquarters of the provincial lords, the castle towns, became the focal points of regional life and bustling commercial centers.

In Edo, Kyoto, and Osaka, as well as the smaller local cities, the development of the currency economy and the distribution network brought into being a substantial body of affluent urban citizens. Throughout the nearly three-hundred years of the Tokugawa period, the taxes levied by the shogun and the provincial lords were largely paid in the form of rice, while the distribution system operated on the basis of cash. This meant that the rice collected as tax had to be converted to cash, and transactions in rice and the money market as a whole took on considerable importance, further enhancing the wealth of the rice brokers and the merchant class in general. In addition, the feudal domains were self-contained economic and political units, which complicated commerce across their boundaries, and here too, the wealthy merchants who acted as middle-men were the beneficiaries.

A rigidly stratified system, artificially dividing the people into four classes—samurai, farmer, artisan, and merchant—was imposed on feudal society. The samurai made up the ruling stratum, and the other three groups constituted the ruled. The samurai were retainers either of the *bakufu* itself or of the *daimyō*, and received stipends in the form of rice which they quickly converted to cash. They were in many respects the white-collar workers of the Tokugawa period. In the absence of war throughout the Tokugawa period, the samurai were less in need of martial prowess than of administrative acumen, and as the centuries of peace wore on, they were gradually molded into a bureaucratized elite.

The farmers were producers of the rice that played the key role in this economy and were the chief taxpayers as well. The artisans were also producers, manufacturing secondary products. The merchants were despised as ranking at the bottom of the social ladder, but in fact had the greatest economic resources at their disposal. Through their control of rice transactions, they exercised substantial hold on the fortunes of even the provincial lords. The most powerful of these merchants were concentrated in Osaka, the center into which poured the produce of land and sea from the prosperous hinterland of western Japan. Practically all goods in western Japan were brought to Osaka first before being distributed to other parts of the country.

Edo was still very much a city under construction, but it could not be derided, for it was the hub and the symbol of the shogunal regime that effectively controlled the country. The Tokugawa *bakufu* adopted as its official political philosophy the Confucian teachings of the Chinese sage Chu Hsi, and this remained the orthodox ideology of Japan throughout the Edo period (1603-1868). Chu Hsi taught that man could achieve the perfection of the sage through deep ethical and philosophical insight. It was the task of the samurai to rise above the farmer, artisan, and merchant and attain spiritual perfection. According to the doctrines of Chu Hsi Confucianism as they were interpreted in Japan, the samurai was supposed to represent the perfected model of humanity the rest of society should emulate. The samurai's stipend was his reward for the performance of his duties as a model member of society.

The tone of the city of Edo was set by the samurai class. Kyoto and Osaka retained leadership in the realm of culture, and at least superficially the new social order was peaceful and stable. A mood affirming the reality of the period of peace and the way of life that sustained that reality spread. The lives of the samurai were governed by the principle of *giri* or social obligation, which was based on the precepts of Confucianism. Every aspect of samurai conduct was determined according to his duty and obligation to society as part of the hierarchy of master-servant relations. For the ruled—the farmers, artisans, and merchants—it was *ninjō*, or human feelings, emotion, and love that weighed the most in human behavior.

The drama inevitably created by the conflicts that emerged between social obligations and personal sentiments was given expression in theatrical form through the *gidayū* puppet plays of Chikamatsu Monzaemon (1653-1724) and depicted in literary form in the novels of Ihara Saikaku (1642-93). Chika-matsu was largely responsible for the establishment of the puppet theater, which had previously been little more than itinerant street entertainment, as a fixed form of urban amusement. His plays include numerous masterpieces on themes taken from history or from important events in the city in his day. Many of the plays are the so-called love-suicide (*shinjū*) stories of lovers who are unable to overcome the brutal realities that keep them apart, and ultimately commit suicide together in the hope that they will attain happiness in the after-life. The love-suicide represented the ideal expression of *ninjō*, natural human feelings, which was the basic principle of action in the common people's world. Plays on historical themes, meanwhile, tended to emphasize the principle of duty. Boldly and candidly, the novelist Saikaku portrayed the duty-bound lives of the samurai as well as the world of the townspeople and their pursuit of money and pleasure.

These themes were also important in other performing arts. Kabuki, which had emerged as a popular form of theater in the sixteenth century, was gradually refined and stylized as performances were adapted to cater to sophisticated urban audiences. Development in Kabuki concentrated on enhancing the stylistic aspects of performances and on portraying the entire spectrum of human feelings and their impact on human society, two characteristics that distinguish this genre even today. Kabuki performances soon gained large and steady audiences and permanent theaters were built in the cities. Sets became more elaborate and professional theater critics emerged. As individual actors established their reputations, Kabuki stars were born. Pictures of famous actors in well-known scenes became favorite themes of woodblock prints, which were a prime medium of communication for low-brow urban culture. The performing arts were rapidly being absorbed into the bulwark of popular culture, and for the people of the cities, the theater was an important form of entertainment.

Another dimension of popular taste was the widespread enthusiasm for reviving the traditions of ancient court culture. By adopting techniques of polychrome decoration in the manufacture of ceramic wares and methods of multi-colored hand-painted and cone dyeing (*yūzen*), people sought to brighten and beautify their drab surroundings. As we noted above, the spaces with which the rich and powerful of the sixteenth century surrounded themselves were lavishly decorated in gold and bright colors. The person who brought this sense of space and design to the world of ceramics was Nonomura Ninsei, who was active in Kyoto in the mid-seventeenth century. Pottery made in Kyoto, in fact, has been famous for its use of multiple colors ever since Nonomura's time. New developments in *yūzen* dyeing, too, helped to stimulate the use of colorful, imaginative designs to the decoration of kimono. It was not long until the wives and daughters of well-off urban citizens were bedecked with bright kimono dyed in many colors and richly decorated with pictorial motifs. Kimono motifs were drawn from favorite themes of nature as well as classical literature, and each held specific associations, serving as an outward expression of the aesthetic sensibility of the wearer. For example, pine, bamboo, plum blossoms, cranes, or turtles, all of which are auspicious symbols of longevity and good fortune, were common motifs used on kimono to be worn on special occasions. This tradition is still very much alive today.

With the increasing attention to beauty and aesthetic refinement in urban life, a new style began to appear in the tea ceremony. Sen no Rikyū's achievements were revived and his place of leadership in the world of tea passed on to his sons. In time, the tea ceremony as Rikyū had taught it attained a position of high respect in society. People looked upon it as a spiritual discipline and a means of creating a special atmosphere within the mundane world of daily life. Just as Zen had done before, the conduct of the tea ceremony in the secluded, separate space of the tea house provided a precious opportunity for solitude and contemplation.

Craftsmen specializing in the design and creation of handcrafted furnishings and utensils for the tea ceremony prospered from the popularity of the tea ceremony. One of these was Nakamura Sōtetsu (1617-95), famous for his lacquered tea canisters and tea scoops. The Nakamura line of craftsmen has been sustained through twelve generations and continues even today to produce fine lacquered tea ceremony utensils.

Portraits

Tokugawa Ieyasu

Kanō Tan'yū

Tokugawa Iemitsu

Tokugawa Ieyasu (1542-1616) ———
The third of the "three great unifiers of Japan," the man who set in place the Tokugawa shogunate, which would last for 265 years. Like his two predecessors Ieyasu hailed from the Nagoya area. The son of a castle lord, he was drawn into the fierce warfare of the times. He faithfully served Nobunaga and then reluctantly submitted to Hideyoshi until the latter's death, when he moved to take power. He won the battle of Sekigahara in 1600 and was appointed shogun three years later. A political genius, he made Edo (Tokyo) his headquarters and from there created a system of military and political checks and balances that effectively controlled Japan's almost 300 feudal lords. The differences between the three unifiers are best expressed in this anecdote: confronted with a caged nightingale that would not sing, Nobunaga would kill the bird; Hideyoshi would try to make it sing; Ieyasu would wait for it to sing.

Kanō Tan'yū (1602-1674) ———
The leading Kanō school painter of his time. The grandson of Kanō Eitoku, Tan'yu restored the position of the Kanō school. He lived in Edo where he did work for Tokugawa shoguns, major temples and vassal lords. Prolific, adept at a variety of styles and a connoisseur of old paintings, Tan'yū produced important works for the Edo, Osaka, Nijō (in Kyoto) and Nagoya Castles, Tōshōgū Shrine in Nikko and Nanzenji Temple in Kyoto. He also left behind a record now invaluable to art historians detailing the many paintings he was asked to authenticate. Tan'yū was the last painter of rank of his school.

See pp.72-73

Tokugawa Iemitsu (1604-1651) ———
Third shogun of the Tokugawa shogunate. Iemitsu, the eldest legitimate son of the second shogun, became shogun in 1623 upon his father's retirement. He managed to survive some court intrigue and by 1631 had the government firmly in hand. Iemitsu was fortunate to have some able men around him upon whose advice he often depended, and during his administration, the Tokugawa government reached the apex of its power and achieved the bureaucratic form it would keep for the next two hundred years. Iemitsu strengthened his rule by stiffening the discipline of the military houses and compelling vassals to reside in Edo in alternate years. He forbid the sale of rice land, intensified the persecution of Christians and instituted a closed-door policy with regard to foreign contact.

Yatsuhashi Kengyō (1614-1685) ———
Famed Japanese harp master who developed a unique style of music named after him. Of provincial origins, Kengyō became a *shamisen* (Japanese musical instrument) artist in Edo, but soon started playing the koto (Japanese harp) and composing music for it. Lured by the city renowned for its historical ties with the koto, Kengyō moved to Kyoto to teach. There he developed his own unique style of koto music which remains classic today.

Nakamura Sōtetsu (1617-1695) ———
Founder of the art of Japanese lacquerware. Little is known of Sōtetsu's early years except that he was born in Kyoto. He developed the first Japanese lacquerware, specializing in tea ceremony

utensils, particularly tea scoops and tea caddies. His family line has continued through twelve generations, serving the Sen family, Kyoto tea ceremony masters, as the designers of their tea utensils.
See p.96

Mitsui Takatoshi (1622-1694) ———
Wealthy merchant who founded what would become the Mitsui financial and industrial conglomerate. The fourth son of a provincial sake brewer and pawnbroker, Takatoshi was successful enough at rice brokering and moneylending to be able to open shops in Edo and Kyoto in 1673. Using what for the times were highly innovative practices—accepting only cash and refusing credit, selling low-priced goods in volume, cutting cloth to length and even holding occasional bargain sales—his shops prospered. Takatoshi introduced the concepts of division of labor and bonuses for productive workers. He set up money exchanges in Edo and Osaka and, in 1691, was appointed a chartered merchant by the shogunate.

Seki Takakazu (1640-1708) ———
The greatest pre-modern Japanese mathematician. Little is known of Seki, though it is believed that this clerk in the shogunal office of clothing and furnishings was a self-educated man. Known as the "Japanese Newton," he developed a method for approximating the roots of a higher-order algebraic equation similar to Newton's. Seki's formulation of the theory of determinants is now generally accepted to have preceded that of the West. Mathematics, however, was not supported by the shogunate and attracted little attention outside of Seki's own students.

Rembrandt Harmensz van Rijn

Corneille, Pierre

Yatsuhashi Kengyō

Molière, Jean-Baptiste Poquelin

Tenzan, part of Seki's "Japanese" algebra, was transmitted secretly and was first published more than fifty years after Seki's death.

Ihara Saikaku (1642-1693) ————
Energetic poet and popular fiction writer whose works are part of the Japanese classical literature canon. Saikaku, the heir of a prosperous Osaka merchant family, began writing poetry in his teens. After the death of his wife in 1675, he left his business in the control of clerks and took up writing in earnest. He wrote comic linked verse and performed many one-man marathon poetry sessions—he once composed 23,500 comic verses in a twenty-four hour span. He made his mark, however, with the publication of *The Life of An Amorous Man* in 1682. During the last ten years of his life Saikaku wrote similar works at a frenzied pace. Love and money were his two great themes which he revealed mostly by poking fun at the rich townsman class and their profligate ways. His colloquial, vernacular style influenced later Japanese writers.
See pp.94-95

Matsuo Bashō (1644-1694) ————
Poet who came near to perfecting the art of haiku. The son of a low-ranking samurai turned farmer, Bashō served a young, literary-minded lord with whom he received training in poetry composition. When his lord died in 1666, Bashō resigned his service and eventually moved to Edo. There he built up a reputation as a poetry teacher. He took up the name Bashō, "banana leaf," and the practice of Zen. In 1684 he went on a journey in search of poetic and spiritual discipline, and thereafter would use

travel to find inspiration. Sprinkled with appropriate haiku, his travel journals were highly polished art forms, the best being his *The Narrow Road to the Deep North*. Bashō's poetic ideals of *sabi*, "a dialectical synthesis of gorgeous and lonely beauty," and *karumi*, "lightness," have become haiku standards.
See pp.76-77

Tokugawa Tsunayoshi (1646-1709) —
The fifth shogun of the Tokugawa shogunate. Nicknamed the "dog shogun" for his many edicts conferring protection and exalted status to dogs, Tsunayoshi largely undid what his father Iemitsu had accomplished, weakening the government through lavish spending and misguided financial legislation. He himself withdrew from the everyday workings of the government, preferring to communicate via his grand chamberlain. He then pursued his interests in literature and the arts, and produced a number of Noh plays in some of which he played a leading role.

Chikamatsu Monzaemon (1653-1724)
Japan's greatest playwright. Chikamatsu's provincial samurai family fled the countryside for Kyoto sometime before he reached age twenty. Although his father had abandoned feudal service, Chikamatsu parlayed his samurai training in Buddhism, Confucianism and Japanese classical literature into a career as a playwright. He began writing for the bunraku puppet theater, but switched almost exclusively to Kabuki. The low position of Kabuki playwrights and the stunning success of his bunraku play *The Love Suicides at Sonezaki* led him to move to Osaka in 1705 and end his years writing bunraku plays based on actual

events and the clash between human emotion and obligation. Chikamatsu, the "Shakespeare of Japan," also wrote the *Kokusenya kassen* (Battles of Coxinga), which ran for seventeen months in an era when plays were changed monthly or sooner.
See pp.78-81

Ogata Kōrin (1658-1716) ————
Rimpa-style painter and designer. Kōrin, the second son of a prosperous and cultivated merchant, squandered his inheritance and had to take up painting to support himself. Kōrin was well educated, having received training in classical ink painting and Japanese drama, and by the 1690s had already designed lacquer boxes that would be widely copied in his own lifetime. Kōrin was awarded a court title, but he moved to Edo in 1704 in search of more lucrative commissions. He was not happy there—his works of this period reveal ominous overtones—and he returned to Kyoto where impoverished, but experiencing a burst of revitalized energy, he lived out his years. Some of his best works date from this last period. The cool elegance of his works is said to have raised the decorative style to perfection.
See pp.86-87

Ichikawa Danjūrō I (1660-1704) ————
The founder of the most illustrious of the major acting family lines in Kabuki. Danjūrō I, influenced by an early form of puppet theater, created the *aragoto* or "dynamic bravado" style of acting which was used particularly in the portrayal of heroes with superhuman powers. The *aragoto* style was widely imitated by Edo performers and became characteristic of Edo Kabuki. A writer of plays under a

Pascal, Blaise

Racine, Jean

Seki Takakazu

pen name, Danjūrō I also starred in the earliest versions of four plays known as "the 18 favorite plays of the Ichikawa family." The family line still continues, Danjūrō XII having received the name during special ceremonies in May 1985. See pp.82-85

Ogata Kenzan (1663-1743) ————
Potter and painter whose imaginative art combined techniques of the Chinese literati-artist tradition with that of the Japanese artist-artisan. Kenzan, the son of a wealthy Kyoto textile merchant, spent his youth in a highly cultured environment, studying Chinese and Japanese poetry. Later he moved near the Ninnaji kiln of a respected potter, eventually taking up a career as an artist. In 1699 he established his own kiln at Narutaki, northwest of Kyoto. His brother Kōrin joined him in a collaborative effort, painting on pottery he had designed, resulting in some of their finest work. A failure as a businessman, Kenzan had to give up his kiln in 1712. He opened a pottery retail shop in Kyoto, and later moved to Edo where he opened a kiln in Kan'eiji Temple ground. See pp.88-89

Sumitomo Tomoyoshi (1670-1719) —
Skillful entrepreneur and merchant. Born the fourth son of a samurai, Tomoyoshi was adopted by the merchant Sumitomo family whose fortune was based on a copper refining technique— learned from a Portugese merchant— which allowed the extraction of its silver content. Tomoyoshi capped this success by acquiring the Besshi copper mine upon which many of the Sumitomo family's later industrial undertakings would be centered. Under Tomoyoshi,

the Sumitomo family was designated the official purveyor of copper to the Toku-gawa shogunate and allowed to become a major exporter of copper.

Kamo no Mabuchi (1697-1769) ———
Poet and *Kokugaku* (Japanese Classics) scholar. The son of a Shinto priest, Mabuchi early on displayed a facility for composing poetry and at the same time excelled in Confucianism and Chinese learning. After studying ethics in Kyoto, Mabuchi went on to Edo where he built up a reputation as a teacher of the classics and was finally asked to teach the shogun's son. He used his political ties to advance the study of the Japanese classics. He believed in the spiritual purity of the *Man'yōshū*, the oldest anthology of Japanese poetry that dated from the seventh century, and he tried to renew interest in a long poetic form found in the *Man'yōshū*, though to no avail. His most enduring and influential work is his scholarly study of the *Manyōshū* wherein he studied each poem intensively from its historical, linguistic and literary aspects.

Ikenobō Senkō II (d. 1659) ————
Famed flower arrangement master of the Ikenobō school. The Ikenobō school was the first school of flower arrangement in Japan. Senkō II was a descendant of the great Sengyō, who created a sensation with an arrangement that initiated the "standing flowers" form of arrangement. Senkō II continued to expand on this form almost two hundred years later. It differed from previous styles which were mere religious offerings. The new art attempted to imitate the grandeur and majesty of nature, eventually obtaining recognition in the form of patronage

from the aristocracy in Senko II's time. The "standing flowers" form harmonized well with the resplendent interiors of the castles of the time. See pp.92-93

Hishikawa Moronobu (?-1694) ———
Pioneer, popularizer and preeminent artist of woodblock prints. Moronobu was the son of a brocade artisan and studied the craft under his father, but left his home in the countryside for Edo after his father's death in 1662. There he became an artist, his earliest works revealing classical training. But, unlike detached genre artists before him— many of whom were without ties to the major schools of painting and labored in anonymity—Moronobu boldly pursued his deep interest in townsman life and insisted on signing his paintings. His style, an effective consolidation of earlier genre paintings and illustrations, was one of controlled, powerful brushstrokes and solid dynamic figures—a style that suited the woodblock medium and laid the groundwork for later woodblock print masters. See pp.74-75

Miyazaki Yūzen (?) ———————
A Kyoto fan-painter who perfected a textile dyeing method that allowed for the first time detailed dyed patterns on textiles. Little is known about Yūzen other than the process which he is said to have developed. The method required the use of rice paste-resist and steaming to dye the cloth following designs that were then washed away in clear, cold river waters. The method was eagerly welcomed when it appeared at the end of the seventeenth century because sumptuary laws prohibited the merchant class from wearing silk.

Newton, Issac

Matsuo Bashō

Bach, Johann S.

Hishikawa Moronobu

Nonomura Ninsei (fl. mid-17th c.) ——— Leading Kyoto ceramic artist in the mid-17th century. Though little is known about his origins, Ninsei probably came from the village of Nonomura in Tamba, an area known for its large tea jars where Ninsei probably did his first work in ceramics. He had studied at the Awata-guchi kilns in Kyoto and in Seto in Aichi prefecture when he was invited to open a kiln at Ninnaji, a Kyoto temple. He accepted, taking part of his name from the temple's name. Ninsei's work ranges in style from simple enamelware and single-glaze pieces to highly decorated enamels of many colors. His pieces, almost all made for the tea ceremony or tea ceremony-related meals, were almost invariably signed with an impressed seal. See pp.90-91

Rembrandt Harmensz van Rijn (1606-1669)
Dutch painter

Corneille, Pierre (1606-1684)
French dramatist

Milton, John (1608-1674)
English poet

Rouchefoucauld, François de la (1613-1680)
French author

Bergerac, Cyrano de (1619-1655)
French poet

La Fontaine (1621-1695)
French poet

Molière, Jean-Baptiste Poquelin (1622-1673)
French dramatist

Pascal, Blaise (1623-1662)
French mathematician, physisist, philosopher

Locke, John (1632-1704)
English philosopher

Spinoza, Baruch (1632-1677)
Dutch philosopher

Wren, Christopher (1632-1723)
English architect

Racine, Jean (1639-1699)
French dramatist

Newton, Issac (1642-1727)
English philosopher, mathematician

Defoe, Daniel (1660-1731)
English author

Swift, Jonathan (1667-1745)
English writer

Couperin, François (1668-1733)
French composer

Peter the Great (1672-1725)
Russian czar

Vivaldi, Antonio (1675?-1741)
Italian composer

Watteau, Jean Antoine (1684-1721)
French painter

Bach, Johann S. (1685-1750)
German composer

Händel, George Frederick (1685-1759)
German composer

Pope, Alexander (1688-1744)
English poet

Montesquieu, Baron de (1689-1755)
French philosopher

Voltaire, François de (1694-1778)
French writer

Hogarth, William (1697-1764)
English painter

Kanō Tan'yū (1602-1674)

This painting of tigers in a bamboo grove on the sliding doors of Nanzenji Temple in Kyoto is one of Tan'yū's most famous works.

74 Moronobu painted this backstage view of the Nakamura-za Kabuki Theater in 1685. Actors are putting on makeup and dressi

さみだれを　あつめてはやし　もがみ川

芭蕉

Against a background of the Mogami River, Bashō's famous haiku poem describing the rainy season reads: "Gathering as it

goes all the rains of June, how refreshing the Mogami flows."

Chikamatsu Monzaemon (1653-1724)

78 This is Chikamatsu in later life against a background of a poem and comments he composed before his death in 1724.

Woodblock print by Kiyonaga depicts two lovers in a scene from *The Love Suicides at Amijima* by Chikamatsu.

80   Chikamatsu's play *The Love Suicides at Sonezaki* deals with the conflict between duty (*giri*) and human affection (*ninjō*).

Ichikawa Danjūrō (1660-1704)

82 Characters with superhuman powers as the one shown here were first created by Danjūrō I.

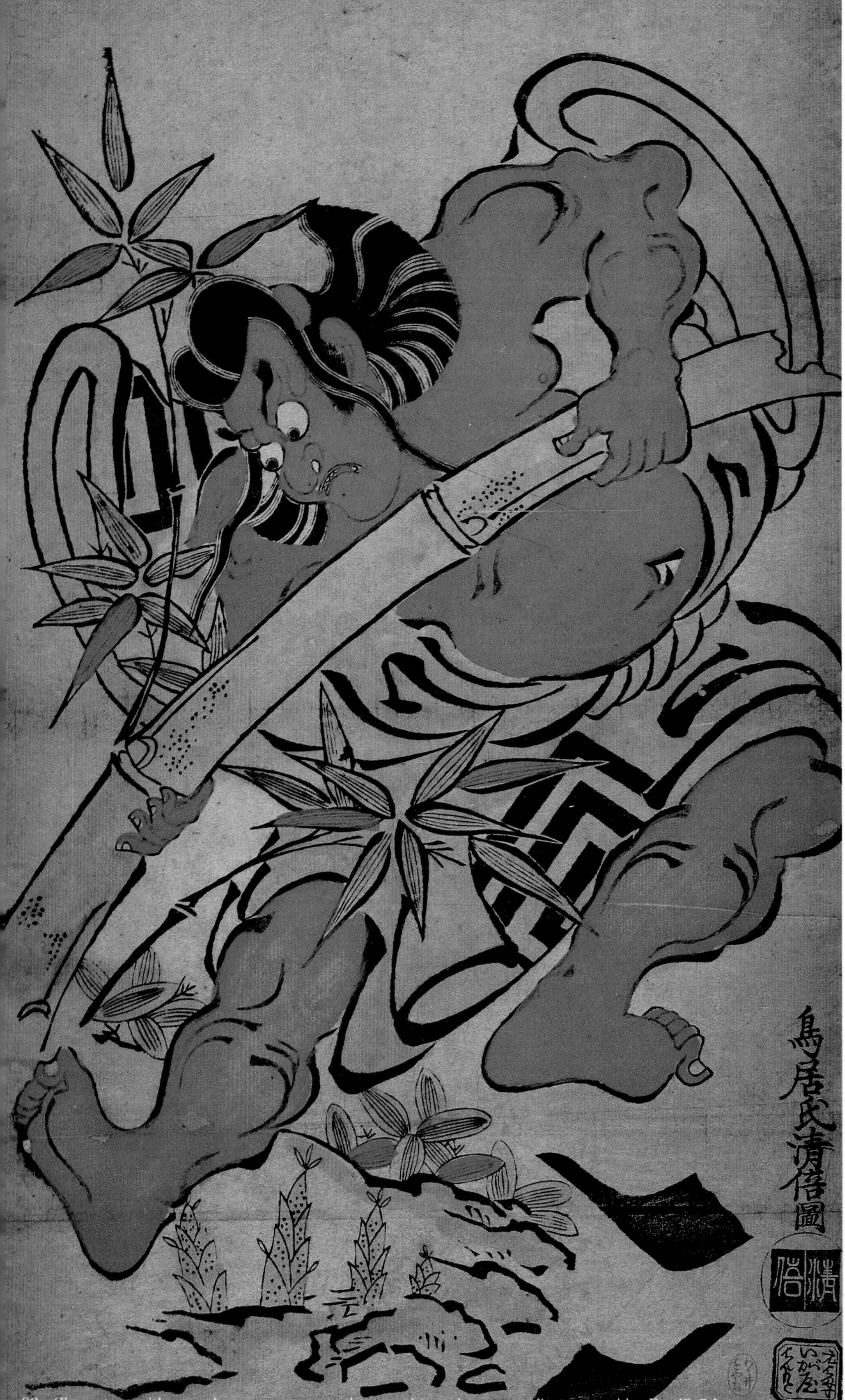

Danjuro I is portrayed in *Shibaraku* (Just a Moment), a play that has become a bravura vehicle of Kabuki.

This is another performance of *Shibaraku* but performed by Danjūrō XII who succeeded to the illustrious family name in 1985.

Ogata Kōrin (1658-1716)

86 Kōrin painted these irises after 1701. Influenced by his training as a textile designer, his paintings were splendidly decorative.

Ogata Kenzan (1663-1743)

88 Kenzan made this set of five dishes with landscape and plant designs in underglaze blue and slip, and overglazed in gold.

Nonomura Ninsei (fl mid-17th century)

Ninsei, a Kyoto ceramic artist of the mid-17th century, created this pheasant-shaped incense burner overglazed with enamel.

Ikenobō Senkō II (d.1659)

Senkō II created this arrangement of narcissuses for Prince Konoe in 1629. The creation was recorded by a painter.

This traditional seven-branch flower arrangement was created by Sen'ei XLV in 1984 at the Nishi-Hongan-ji Temple in Kyoto. *93*

Ihara Saikaku (1642-1693)

94 Saikaku shaved his head when his wife died in 1675 and devoted himself entirely to haiku and prose.

The gate to Shimabara, the pleasure quarter in Kyoto that Saikaku frequented and described in his novels   95

Nakamura Sōtetsu (1617-1695)

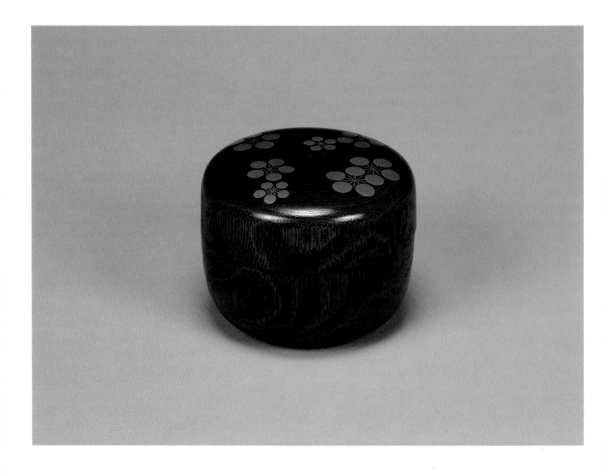

The lacquerwork master Sōtetsu I created this clear lacquer, gold-decorated tea caddy for a tea ceremony master.

18th Century

By the eighteenth century, Edo was a large city and thriving political and economic center. Kyoto and Osaka, too, were growing metropolises, each developing its own distinctive cultural flavor. Edo, which for centuries had remained culturally subordinate to the older cities in the Kansai area, now had a population of 1.2 million and a lively culture of its own. The population of Japan as a whole at this time was approximately 30 million.

The castle towns in the provinces also grew, but, in contrast to the pluralistic life of the big cities, where people from all over the country mingled, they were relatively sequestered towns where culture became increasingly ingrown and regionally specific. The rich regional diversity of Japanese culture even today is the legacy of the development that went on within each of the feudal domains. There was also tremendous variety among the different sections of the large cities, where distinctive value systems prevailed. After more than a century of peace, culture had become exceedingly intensive and diversified.

At the same time, though the social system was superficially just as rigid as it had always been, there began to appear signs of considerable internal flux. Many of the provincial lords set up schools within their domains, and private academies were founded in the cities. By learning and studying Confucianism it was possible to gain admittance to the new profession of teacher. The concentration of population in the cities intensified the need for medical doctors, and the growth of commerce meant that skill in mathematics was in great demand. For the people of the cities, three skills became indispensable: reading, writing, and the use of the abacus. Scholarship provided the pathway to a new occupation that did not fall neatly into the rigid class system of feudal society. Gradually a new intelligentsia emerged in the cities distinct from both the old leisure classes—the upper-echelon samurai and wealthy merchants—that was composed of professional intellectuals, including medical doctors and teachers.

As the ranks of the leisure class grew, the livelihood of professional painters—who specialized in the ornamentation of the interiors and furnishings of the wealthy—became assured. The traditional genre of Chinese-style painting maintained a large following, but other, less stylized approaches to painting began to appear as well. In contrast to the formalism of the Northern School of Chinese painting, artists of the so-called Southern School (*nanga*) became active who depicted conceptual dynamics spontaneously and who were more interested in symbolism and poesy than pictorial realism. This school became established as the *bunjinga* or "literati" style of painting. Nevertheless, painters in the realistic style continued to be active. Artists now appeared in every class in society, and their themes were no longer confined to traditional subjects, but focused on nature and everyday life.

In addition to the traditional school of painting, popular genre art also began to flourish. Paintings in this style were called "pictures of the floating world"—*ukiyoe*—and reproduced in woodblock print form, they were widely circulated. At first they were monochrome, but it was not long before techniques for making polychrome prints were devised, and ukiyoe became synonymous with color prints. The ukiyoe artists depicted popular actors and famed beauties of the day, and the prints served as the medium by which fashions and topics of interest spread among the populace. Most ukiyoe were made in Edo and they were popular not only among residents but coveted by visitors to the city as souvenirs.

In the eighteenth century, Kabuki, which was among the favorite subjects of ukiyoe art, shifted away from the themes of *giri* and *ninjō* and began to portray the cultural decadence that was spreading throughout the maturing urban society. Plays dealing with the erotic, the grotesque, and the mysterious, as well as the exploits of heroic outlaws enjoyed the greatest popularity. Where once the characters of the plays had been chiefly of merchant origin, now the protagonists included thieves and hunted men and people from the pleasure quarters, and this new content of Kabuki drew yet larger audiences.

The improvement of stage mechanisms also contributed to the development of Kabuki. The unique revolving stage for changing scenes and the lift and trap door by which an actor can be raised up onto the stage or disappear beneath it were devised and stage properties became increasingly complex. These mechanisms were instrumental in the shift of the Kabuki theater from stylization to realism.

The trend toward action and realism and treatment of contemporary themes gave the Kabuki theater appeal among audiences from a broader spectrum of society. But people's appetite for sentimental diversion also turned in the direction of literature, and the popular novel was born. The new popular fiction dealt with many themes, from historical sagas to realistic accounts of the life of Edo townspeople to tales of the "floating world" of the pleasure quarters. Novels took up every facet of urban life, usually small volumes printed by the woodblock method. Some were amply illustrated, often in full color. The publishing industry in Edo, Kyoto, and Osaka in the eighteenth century flourished, making available not only popular fiction, but dictionaries, poetry and haiku collections, as well as works on science, religion, and other non-fiction subjects. Then, as today, the love of reading that is a characteristic of Japanese culture was by no means confined to the intellectual elite. It was during the Edo period that writers of fiction enjoyed professional recognition for the first time, among them Takizawa Bakin (1767-1848), known for his moralistic and serious works, and Tamenaga Shunsui (1789-?), a writer of romances.

The cities offered a wide variety of entertainments, both temporary and permanent, including freak shows and itinerant side-shows presenting various kinds of feats and entertainments. The atmosphere was much like the market-town fairs of Europe such as the famous Bartholomew Fair of London. The townspeople also had an inordinate fondness for taking in the seasonal sights of nature, especially the cherry-blossoms in the spring and the turning of the maple leaves in autumn. So popular were excursions for this purpose that in Edo it was a *bakufu* policy to promote the planting of cherry and maple trees, and artificially created grounds for cherry-blossom viewing were set aside. Parks built for this purpose and later maintained and supported by the *bakufu* itself include those at Koganei and Asukayama in Tokyo. In provincial cities as well, there are many areas where cherry or maple trees were planted long ago in order to enhance the pleasures of the spring and autumn seasons. The custom among urban citizens of dressing up gaily for a picnic beneath the cherry blossoms or where brightly colored autumn foliage can be viewed to best advantage thus goes back to the Edo period.

The townspeople's love of excursions eventually led to extended travels around the country by foot.

From about the middle of the seventeenth century, increasing numbers from the leisure classes began to take to the roads in search of picturesque landscapes. Wherever fine landscapes or sites famous in history or literature were to be found, there the travellers gathered. For many urban dwellers, a sightseeing tour to Kyoto or Edo or a pilgrimage to the Grand Shrine at Ise might be the journey of a lifetime. Pilgrimages to Ise Shrine were generally conducted in groups, often organized by pre-modern travel agents. Many people also joined group tours to major shrines and temples both in the provinces and in Kyoto.

The popularization of travel served to turn people's interests toward landscapes and conditions in the countryside outside of the city in which they lived. Their fascination in the rural landscape nurtured a new group of landscape artists who appeared in the eighteenth century, including Hokusai (1760-1849) and Hiroshige (1797-1858). Their prints, which captured views of familiar landscapes found along major routes of travel well-known even to city residents from unusual or striking perspectives were vastly popular. Illustrated guidebooks to famous places around the countryside were also published in large numbers. One of the best-sellers among these was *Miyako meisho zue* (Celebrated Places in Kyoto) consisting of a series of scenes from the ancient capital.

After nearly three hundred years of peace under the rigid feudal society, Japan's indigenous culture was nearing the point of maturation and decadence. At this crucial juncture, influences from the outside world, both east and west, began to flow into the country once more. The cultural leaders were the first to be alerted to these outside forces. They quickly realized that it was not weird and inhuman creatures that inhabited the world outside of Japan but other human beings with rich and diverse cultures of their own. Japan was not the whole world, and widening awareness of other civilizations decisively shaped nineteenth-century Japan. As that awareness spread, Japan's cities ceased to be closed, inwardly oriented cultural realms, but turned 180 degrees to face outward to the West and Western civilization.

Portraits

Tokugawa Yoshimune

Franklin, Benjamin

Rousseau, Jean Jacques

Tokugawa Yoshimune (1684-1751) — Eighth shogun of the Tokugawa shogunate and government reformer. Yoshimune was the vassal lord of a minor domain when he was chosen, at 32, to become the shogun upon the extinction of the main line of the Tokugawa family. One of the most talented of the fifteen Tokugawa shoguns, he brought to the office an awareness of how the common people lived, yet in spite of this provincial touch, he was adept at political maneuvering in the capital. He instituted reforms aimed at restoring the shogunate and samurai class to financial solvency. Yoshimune disdained the luxuries his position could obtain preferring to live simply, and he also tried to restore samurai moral and fitness by reviving martial activities and sports. He also allowed—and encouraged—the importation of Western books, except ones on Christianity, and increased production of agricultural goods and commodities through a system of detailed record-keeping.

Itō Jakuchū (1716-1800) — Painter known for his renderings of exotic birds. Jakuchū, the eldest son of a prosperous Kyoto greengrocer, turned over the family business to his brother in 1755 in order to become a painter. Jakuchū specialized in meticulously detailed, almost surrealistic depictions of exotic birds and fowl. Legend has it that Jakuchū, loath to rely on conventional painting formulas, kept a collection of the birds in his own yard. He spent the last forty years of his life on two massive projects, the first, thirty large scrolls painted as a votive offering to a temple, and the other, an outdoor mural series of

the eight stages of the Buddha's life. See pp.104-105

Tanuma Okitsugu (1719-1788) — Controversial shogunate official. Tanuma rose to power unprecedented for a man of humble origins. Having entered government service as a page, he eventually served as senior councillor and grand chamberlain concurrently. He was responsible for implementing programs that led to greater centralization: the licensing of commercial agents and monopoly associations, extending shogunate control over commodities, and setting up a silver coin mint and a loan fund to assist debt-ridden vassal lords. Tanuma implemented an aggressive economic policy that encouraged expanding reclaimed rice paddy land and other measures whose aim was to increase tax revenues. He was the first to recognize the value of northern Japan, ordering a survey of that area. His position depended on his influence with the shogun and he fell quickly from favor when the shogun died. His successors vilified him and his name is now synonymous with evil.

Ike no Taiga (1723-1776) — Artist and calligrapher who established a uniquely Japanese literati style of painting. Taiga, the son of a farmer who ended up working at the silver mint in Kyoto, was a child prodigy who by age six had already awed monks at Mampukuji Temple with his calligraphic ability. He studied under a variety of influential teachers, learning, for example, the method of painting with his fingernails instead of a brush. When he opened a shop in Kyoto to sell fans, he crossed the boundary from amateur to professional,

breaking with Chinese tradition. The majority of his works are landscapes ranging in style from the simple to the elaborate and from Chinese to Japanese. See pp.106-107

Miura Baien (1723-1789) — Philosopher and educator. Born into a medical family in Kyushu, Baien developed an absorbing interest in Chinese, Indian and Japanese philosophies, Neo-Confucianism, natural science, ethics and economics—instead of in medicine. He eventually turned his family home into a private school. Baien encouraged open discussion, accepted students regardless of age, class, sex or legal status, called his students "friends," "brothers," or "gentlemen" and, in the case of poorer students, provided them with food and clothing. He followed Confucian tenets, living a frugal life and giving away his savings. Baien viewed the universe in terms of a universal principle he called *jōri* based on a dialectic similar to Hegel's and believed that all beings and other phenomena arose from the interaction of sets of opposites.

Suzuki Harunobu (1725-1770) — The first woodblock print artist to produce full-color prints. Harunobu's origins are almost unknown, though he was probably from Edo since his earliest works portray Edo style Kabuki actors. He worked on calendars in 1765 and 1766 and, around this time, first developed the full-color print which greatly changed woodblock artistry. Working primarily for a samurai clientele, Harunobu produced hundreds of single-sheet color prints, twenty illustrated books and a number of paintings on a variety of

Tanuma Okitsugu

Miura Baien

Kant, Immanuel

Motoori Norinaga

subjects including whimsical views of classical subjects. He was also known for his prints of beautiful women in dream-like settings.

See pp.110-111

Motoori Norinaga (1730-1801) ———
Kokugaku (Japanese Classics) scholar. Norinaga, the son of a prominent dealer in cotton goods was ten when his father died, but he received a wide-ranging education under his mother's care. He was temporarily adopted by another merchant family, but disliked business and returned home. His mother then sent him to Kyoto to study medicine. There he became versed in the Chinese classics and Japanese poetry. He returned to his provincial home six years later and began practicing medicine while writing and lecturing evenings on the classics. He started work on his magnum opus, 44 volumes of the first comprehensive study of the *Kojiki*, Japan's oldest extant book which Norinaga revered as the basis of Japanese culture. The work took 34 years to complete and is still highly regarded today.

Maruyama Ōkyo (1733-1795) ———
Painter and founder of the Maruyama school of painting. Despite the poverty of his farming family, Ōkyo was sent as a youth to study painting in Kyoto where he studied a variety of techniques, including Western-derived and Chinese techniques. He believed in working from sketches of life and mixed realistic perspective and chiaroscuro with traditional and decorative techniques, winning enthusiastic praise. His works were widely copied and numerous forgeries appeared as well. Although Ōkyo was a

master of many styles, his forte was his rendition of flowers and trees.

See pp.108-109

Sugita Gempaku (1733-1817) ———
Physician and the first translator of a Western anatomical text. The son of a physician, Gempaku was influenced by Dutch doctors he met in Edo and, after observing an autopsy of a beheaded criminal and realizing that standard Japanese anatomical texts were incorrect, he and a group of colleagues began translating a Dutch anatomical text. Aware of the government's anti-Western bias, Gempaku submitted pre-publication copies to officials, and received shogunal approval. His textbook, illustrated by woodblock prints, appeared in 1774.

See pp.114-115

Inō Tadataka (1745-1818) ———
Geographical surveyor who was the first to use modern scientific surveying methods to produce the extraordinarily accurate maps known as the "Inō maps." Born on the coast of Chiba prefecture, Tadataka was adopted into a prosperous rice-dealing and brewing family at seventeen. He studied calendar-making and astronomy on his own, however, and at 49 left his family to go to Edo to study map-making and astronomy. After joining a 180-day surveying trip of Ezo (now Hokkaido) for the shogunate, he was ordered to survey the coasts of the main island of Japan. He died at 73 before completing his work and it was finished by his students and friends.

See pp.112-113

Shiba Kōkan (1747-1818) ———
Artist, writer and pioneer in the Westernization of Japan. Born in Edo, Kōkan

was trained in traditional painting techniques. He opposed the conservative Tokugawa government, envisioning a social order similar to that of the West. He produced some Western-style oil paintings and, in 1783, his first copperplate etchings based on techniques he had learned from a Dutch encyclopedia. In 1788 he traveled to Nagasaki seeking further contact with Western learning. He was a prolific writer, publishing works on astronomy, geography, Western painting, and Dutch culture as well as the journal of his Nagasaki trip. He became disillusioned in old age.

See p.129

Kitagawa Utamaro (1753-1806) ———
Creative and influential woodblock print artist whose prints of women marked the apex of this genre. Utamaro studied with a minor artist of the Kanō school, but his talents unfolded only gradually, becoming apparent when he had reached his mid-thirties. His earliest works were illustrations for cheap popular books, but by the end of the 1770s, he was producing superb prints as well as designing beautiful illustrated books on the history of woodblock prints. In spite of this work, Utamaro's fame rests on his renditions of women of all classes in a never-ending variety of poses which reveal their personalities and moods. By the 1790s, he was the most emulated of woodblock print artists.

See pp.116-117

Tsuruya Namboku (1755-1829) ———
Noted Kabuki playwright. The son of an Edo dyer, Namboku frequented nearby Kabuki theaters in his youth. By age twenty, he had given up his father's trade and apprenticed himself to a group of

Washington, George

Goethe, Johann Wolfgang von

Mozart, Wolfgang Amadeus

playwrights. Known in his heyday as "Namboku the Great," he created a new type of Kabuki drama that depicted the world of the townsman. Namboku's dramas portray a society devoid of ethics, whose members are driven by an unquenchable lust or thirst for money and power. His characters, often those who have fallen from social status, argue in a mixture of refined language and the coarsest types of speech, amidst brothels, cemeteries and other unsavory places.

See pp.118-119

Katsushika Hokusai (1760-1849) ——
One of the most famous woodblock print artists, known for his views of Mt. Fuji. Hokusai's origins are obscure, but he was adopted by a craftsman family whose head was the official mirror-maker for the shogunate. Although he displayed talent for painting at an early age, he did not excel until his late thirties, when he became known for a variety of works—woodblock prints, paintings, illustrations, commercial fiction—which he produced under several noms de plume. He did not produce his masterpieces, prints of views of Mt. Fuji in particular and of waterfalls, bridges, birds and ghosts, until he reached his seventies. Until Hokusai painted Mt. Fuji, this symbol of Japan had drawn little attention from Japanese painters who were steeped in Chinese traditions.

See pp.124-125

Raiden Tameemon (1767-1825) ——
Sumo wrestler of enormous strength and popularity. The son of a provincial tenant farmer, Raiden drew attention because of his size and strength. Raiden,

whose name consists of the Chinese characters meaning "thunder" and "lightning," moved from his village to Edo where he became a professional wrestler. He was promoted to sumo's second highest rank in 1795 and lost but one match in the ensuing sixteen years until his retirement. There is speculation that he was denied the highest position in sumo for political reasons.

See p.128

Takizawa Bakin (1767-1848) ——
Writer, critic and diarist known for his moralistic prose fiction. Bakin resigned the duties of a fifth son of a low-ranking samurai to become a townsman intent upon supporting himself by writing. Bakin wrote chapbooks while apprenticing under a popular writer of the time. He turned to romances based on ancient myths and legends and, between 1808 and 1813, became recognized as Edo's leading writer. His didactic pieces attempt to explain ethical values such as filial piety, loyalty, chastity and self-lessness, and preached that "virtue is rewarded and vice punished." His masterpiece, *Satomi and the Eight Dogs*, took 28 years, appearing periodically. Its theme, the restoration of a samurai family, might have been his own wish, one dashed by the early death of his only son.

See pp.120-121

Tamenaga Shunsui (1790-1843) ——
Writer whose works mark the acme of the "human emotions" genre. Little is known of Shunsui's early life except that he was the son of an Edo merchant. He studied under some popular writers and then in 1821 founded a publishing firm which printed some previously pub-

lished material. Outrage against this piracy led Shunsui into writing himself though many of his books of the next ten years are admitted plagiarisms or were written by assistants. Nevertheless, in 1832 he produced *Plum Calendar*, a superb work that was almost modern in its language. The work revealed feelings and motivations that had long been repressed in Japan.

Andō Hiroshige (1797-1858) ——
Woodblock print artist best known for his landscapes. Hiroshige's family exemplifies the mobility of the Edo era: his great grandfather was a steward in service to a samurai lord; his grand-father, an archery instructor in Edo; and his father, a fireman. Hiroshige himself inherited the fireman's stipend—and duties—at age 12 when his parents died, but his interest was in painting. He investigated new techniques that gave landscapes an added energy, subjects not part of the woodblock tradition. He used shadowing and a full range of coloring to invest new life into the woodblock genre. In 1832 he relinguished his fireman's duties to his son and then, working devotedly, produced his most famous work, *Fifty-Three Stations along the Tokaido*, views of Japan's most important thoroughfare that linked Kyoto and Edo.

See pp.126-127

Utagawa Kuniyoshi (1797-1861) ——
Woodblock print artist known for his bold, startingly original works. The son of a silk dyer, Kuniyoshi was apprenticed to the leading artist of the time before he was thirteen. By seventeen, he was studying diligently on his own, spurred, according to anecdote, by a snub from

Beethoven, Ludwig van

Napoléon I

Tamenaga Shunsui

Andō Hĩroshige

his teacher's top pupil. Eventually he developed an individual style that would be copied by his rivals. His forte was the depiction of heroic scenes which were innovative and popular. He went on to produce prints and drawings of landscapes, women, cats and ghosts. Kuniyoshi's works reveal vigor and versatility.

Courtesan Yatsuhashi (fl. 1800) ——— Top ranking courtesan of the Yoshiwara red light district in Edo who was immortalized in a Kabuki play. Yoshiwara was the most famous of the licensed quarters allowed by government regulation at the beginning of the Edo era (1600-1868). It was during one of Yoshiwara's grand spectacles—a parade of the high-class courtesans in all their splendor—that a rich farmer from the country fell in love with Yatsuhashi. But the farmer, with his ugly, pockmarked face, came to feel humiliated by Yatsuhashi and the people of the quarter, and he killed Yatsuhashi.This episode became the basis for a well-knqwn Kabuki play.
See pp.122-123

Tōshūsai Sharaku ——————
(active mid-1794-early-1795)
Woodblock print artist known for his portraits of Kabuki actors. Sharaku is an anomaly, an artist who had a short burst of productivity and popularity before disappearing until Westerners discovered him a hundred years later. Sharaku's earliest and most important work is a series of 28 large half-length portraits of 30 Kabuki actors printed on dark mica backgrounds. The portraits, probably a set, showed the actors in roles at three major Edo Kabuki theaters.
See p.128

Franklin, Benjamin (1706-1790)
American statesman

Johnson, Samuel (1709-1784)
English author

Rousseau, Jean Jacques (1712-1778)
French philosopher

Diderot, Denis (1713-1784)
French encyclopedist

Smith, Adam (1723-1790)
English economist

Kant, Immanuel (1724-1804)
German philosopher

Catherine II (the Great) (1729-1796)
Russian empress

Washington, George (1732-1799)
First U.S. president

Haydn, Josef (1732-1809)
Austrian composer

Paine, Thomas (1737-1809)
American author

Goya, Francisco de (1746-1828)
Spanish painter

Goethe, Johann Wolfgang von (1749-1832)
German writer

Mozart, Wolfgang Amadeus (1756-1791)
Austrian composer

Blake, William (1757-1827)
English artist, mystic, poet

Schiller, Johann Friedrich von (1759-1805)
German dramatist

Malthus, Thomas Robert (1766-1834)
English economist

Napoléon I (1769-1821)
French emperor

Hegel, G.W.F. (1770-1831)
German philosopher

Beethoven, Ludwig van (1770-1827)
German composer

Wordsworth, William (1770-1850)
English writer

Austen, Jane (1775-1817)
English novelist

Turner, Joseph (1775-1851)
English painter

Stephenson, George (1781-1848)
English inventor and founder of railways

Schopenhauer, Arthur (1788-1860)
German philosopher

Byron, Lord (1788-1824)
English poet

Rossini, Gioacchino (1792-1868)
Italian composer

Keats, John (1795-1821)
English poet

Heine, Heinrich (1797-1856)
German poet

2/04 This painting by Jakuchū shows vibrant patterns and meticulous attention to detail.

The Kintai Bridge in Yamaguchi prefecture by Ike no Taiga

Itsukushima Shrine in Hiroshima prefecture by Ike no Taiga

Ōkyo's realistic sketch of butterflies shows his keen observation of nature. He created this work in 1776.

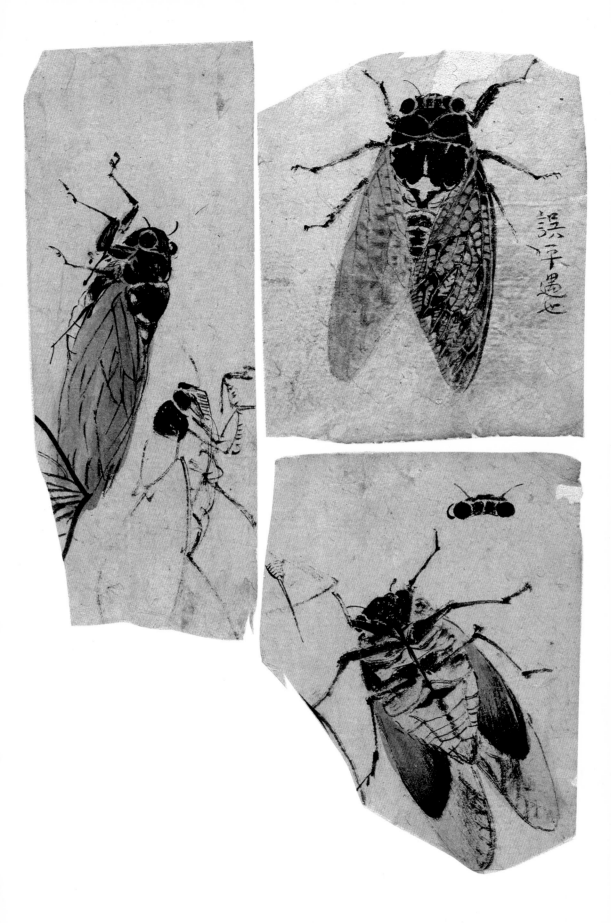

These cicadas sketched by Ōkyo reflect the influence of western techniques of realism and of Chinese paintings. 109

Harunobu's polychrome print of woman at loom and watching child against a red background

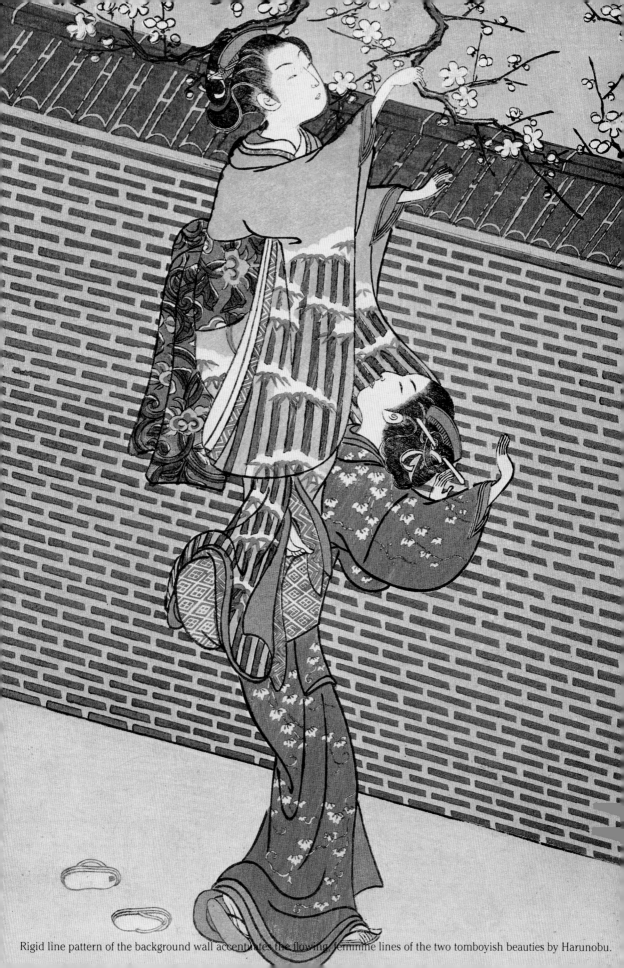

Rigid line pattern of the background wall accentuates the flowing, feminine lines of the two tomboyish beauties by Harunobu.

Inō Tadataka (1745-1818)

112 Portrait of the geographical surveyor Tadataka in his late years. By the age of 70, he had spent 3,737 days surveying.

Tadataka's map of western Japan. Aki (in middle of upper center grid) is today's Hiroshima. *113*

114 Gempaku, physician and scholar of western learning, portrayed at the age of 80 by Ishikawa Tairo in 1812

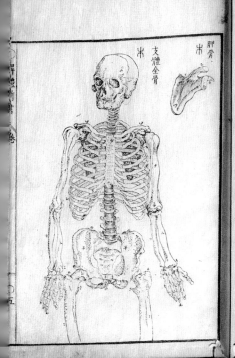

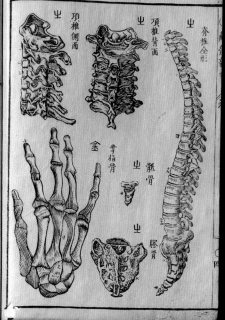

脊椎全形

項椎背面

項椎側面

背相骨

瓶骨

膝骨

金

胛骨

支體全骨

解體新書卷之一

日本

官醫　東都桂川甫周世民閱

東都石川玄常世通參

同藩中川淳庵鱗校

若狹杉田玄白翼譯

○解體大意篇第一

○夫解體之書、所以解體之法也。蓋說形體
之名狀、及諸臟之內外。一身之主用矣。

欲其審之者、無如直割見屍。其次、無如割

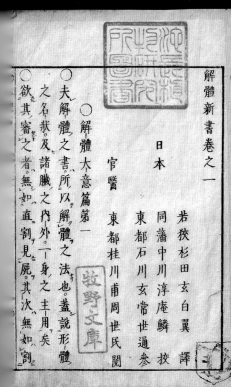

Kitagawa Utamaro (1753-1806)

116   This woodblock print by Utamaro is titled *Needlework*. It shows women working at home on a summer's day.

118   A scene from *The Scarlet Princess of Edo*, the masterpiece by the Kabuki playwright Namboku as performed in the United

Takizawa Bakin (1767-1848)

Copies of Bakin's historical romance *Satomi and the Eight Dogs* comprising 106 volumes which took him 28 years to complete

臺玉藤原中行行畫

Portrait of Bakin, the son of a low-ranking samurai who resigned his duties to become a writer, critic and diarist *121*

Courtesan Yatsuhashi (fl 1800)

竹治

小尾張

A scene from a Kabuki play about the famous courtesan Yatsuhashi (in center) in the licensed quarter of Yoshihara. At left

the rich, pockmarked farmer who fell in love with her but later killed her believing he had been humiliated.

Katsushika Hokusai (1760-1849)

The famous woodblock print by Hokusai titled *The Great Wave at Kanagawa* is one of his "36 Views of Mt. Fuji."

Andō Hiroshige (1797-1858)

Selected scenes from the "53 Stations of the Tokaido Road" from Nihombashi in Edo to Kyoto by Hiroshige

Raiden Tameemon (1767-1825)

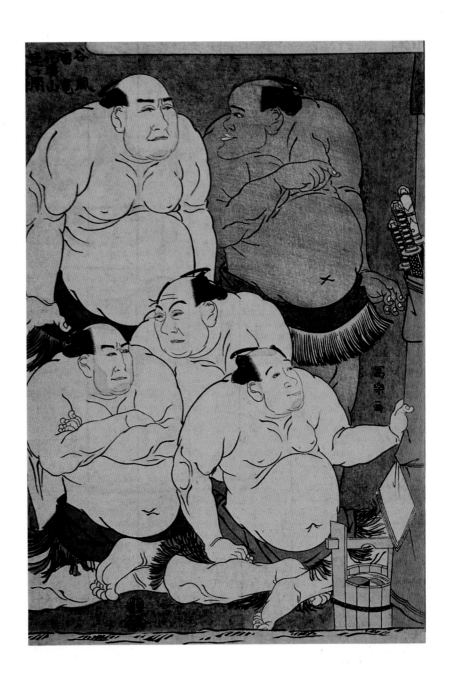

Sumo wrestlers by Sharaku, with the famous sumo champion Raiden at upper right

A copperplate etching of "The Celestial Sphere" by Shiba Kōkan who copied it from a Dutch engraving in 1796.

Notes

Text by Yoshida Mitsukuni
Translated by
Lynne E. Riggs
Captions by the editorial staff
"Portraits" by Jorge Ribeiro
and Carol Simons

Editor: Sesoko Tsune
Art Director: Tanaka Ikko
Designer: Kinoshita Katsuhiro
              Kaneko Seigo
Editorial Supervisor: Ken Ishii
Editorial Assistants: Mizukami Machiko
                      Kondoh Ryuji
                      Sawada Naoko
                      Imaizumi Akiko

Published by Mazda Motor Corporation
Printed by Dai Nippon Printing Co., Ltd.
Printed in Japan

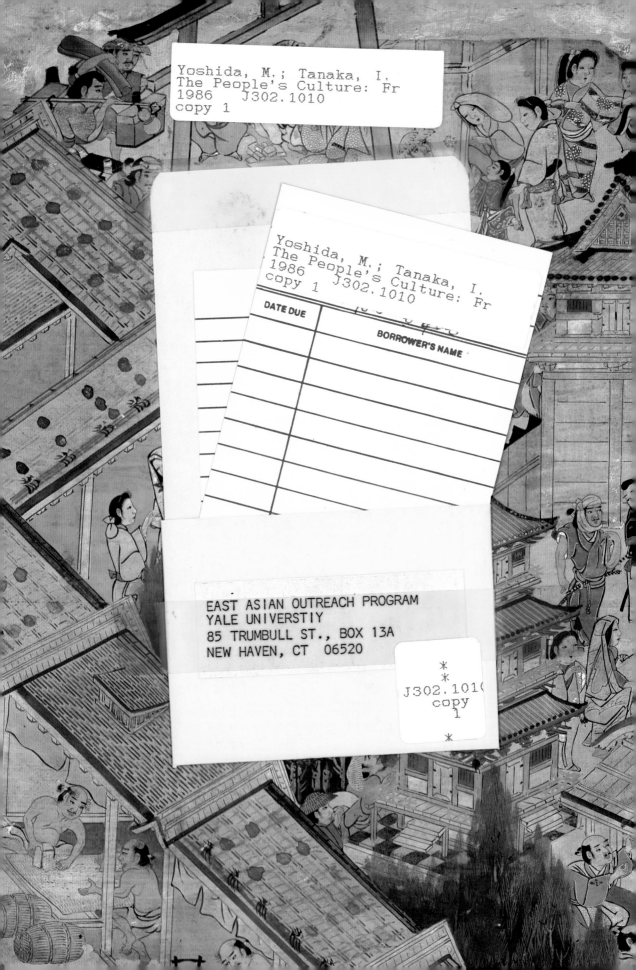